$uccessful Hotel $ales in 5 Easy $teps

Dr. Tony Alessandra
Dr. Joseph "Mick" La Lopa

PLATINUM RULE PRESS

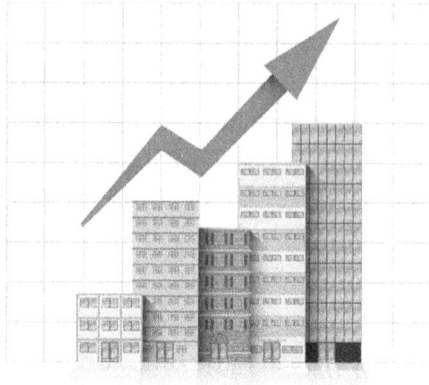

$uccessful Hotel $ales in 5 Easy $teps

Dr. Tony Alessandra and Dr. Joseph La Lopa

ISBN: 0-000000-00-0 (Hardcover)

ISBN: 978-0-9819371-2-0 (Paperback)

ISBN: 0-000000-00-0 (Audio)

ISBN: 0-000000-00-0 (eBook)

Published by:

✚ PLATINUM RULE PRESS

Cover & Interior Design by: Glenn Griffiths

1-619-610-9933

www.assessments24x7.com/the-platinum-rule.asp

REVIEWERS COMMENTS ABOUT THIS BOOK

"This book is a great reminder that it always starts by getting to know each individual. Too often salespeople go through the check list without ever truly understanding the customer's needs. Practicing adaptability not only helps us win more business, but also makes sure we are doing all we can to help each customer – and the colleagues we lead – to be their very best."
– **Pete Sears**, Group President Americas, Hyatt

This book is one of the first of its kind that correlates the traits of salespeople to the traits of customers and tailors it specifically to the hospitality industry! Successful hotel salespeople today MUST know how to effectively interact with their customers and their colleagues."
– **Robert Gilbert,**President & CEO, Hospitality Sales & Marketing Association International

"This book is a great roadmap to a successful interaction with top sales prospects. It is also extremely useful in life – it is a helpful guide to interacting with those who are like you, and those who are not. I highly recommend it."
– **Robert Dora**, CEO Dora Hospitality,

"It is not often you find a book everyone can apply daily to both their professional and personal lives to get ahead"
– **Javaud Mushtaq**, Executive Consultant, Hospitality Sales & Marketing

"I was a student and teaching assistant for Dr. La Lopa in his sales class at Purdue. Since graduating, the lessons learned have helped me to enhance both my personal life and professional career; the tools I learned also help to guide my staff in exceeding their own objectives."
– **Ryan Harris**, PMP, PMI-ACP VP Marketing @ Rocket Gaming

ACKNOWLEDGEMENTS

We first want to thank to thank those sales professionals who reviewed this book, as noted on the previous page. They were instrumental in helping make this book a great sales tool for hotel salespeople.

We are grateful to all of the psychologists, sociologists, visionaries, philosophers, coaches, consultants, trainers, speakers and authors who directly and indirectly influenced our work, documented their findings, and crafted foundations of evidence upon which we could build.

We wish to thank our clients for providing us with encouragement, financial support, opportunities to fail forward (and grow in the process) and for challenging our thinking.

We acknowledge Marc Brett, one time corporate sales recruiter for Hilton Hotels for providing the essay for hotel sales 101.

We extend a special thanks to Glenn Griffiths for the wonderful graphic design he provided for the cover and contents of this book.

DEDICATIONS

I dedicate this book to my late father, Victor Alessandra, who taught me the "street smarts" that helped me become successful in selling, in business and in life.

– Tony Alessandra

This book is dedicated to my father and mother for their unconditional love and support as I found my way in the world. I also dedicate this book to my wife and children, who inspire me every day to be a better person, father, husband, and teacher.

– Mick La Lopa

TABLE OF CONTENTS

INTRODUCTION

Hotel salespeople have good weeks and they have bad weeks just like anyone in the sales profession. When they have good weeks, they naturally attribute it to their sales prowess and the bad weeks are blamed on customers who were just too difficult to please. What if the success or failure of any given sale is based on the luck of the draw? Perhaps a successful sale is made when the customer happens to buy the way the salesperson sells. Conversely, the lost sale may have been due to a mismatch in the way the salesperson sells compared to the way the customer buys. The bottom line is that the salesperson is the primary reason there are good days and bad days. Selling to customers the way THEY prefer to buy will lead to greater sales.

Most hotel salespeople are taught only one way to sell their hotel to customers in their primary social, military, educational, religious, fraternal (SMERF) markets. A standard checklist is used for each customer within those market segments with no regard for the differences in how customers buy hotel services for themselves and others. Customer A walks in the door and the sales team is taught to run down the checklist to learn more about the customer's needs and wants. Then is given the obligatory routine tour of the entire property—instead of being shown the specific way the hotel may satisfy the customer's needs and wants. Customer B walks in the door; they get the same treatment as A. Customer C walks in the door, gets the same treatment as B, and the pattern continues.

1

Do you see the problem? Customers are not clones; they are all different and when their differences are recognized salespeople are more successful. Their reasons for doing business with a hotel may be different and so is the way in which they buy. We are not talking about differences in personality, occupation, status, or market segment. We are talking about differences in behavioral styles which, when recognized, will increase the probability of a sale.

This book will give you a clear indication of how your natural selling style (based on your behavioral style) connects you with **one** of the four buying styles. Then you will learn how to adapt your selling style to connect with the other three styles (the ones that you may have been losing as customers).

When you learn to adapt your selling style to each customer's buying style, you will be a highly successful salesperson because your customers will like you, buy from you and refer others to you.

The $uccessful Hotel $ales in 5 Easy $teps book is based on a matching process: matching the right service to the corresponding set of customer needs, matching the sales pace to the customer's buying pace, and matching your selling style to the buying style of every customer. The ability to adapt your style to your customer's styles helps you build rapport and develop strong relationships.

Your internal voice may be whispering to you, "Isn't it being manipulative when a sales professional adjusts his or her style to match a customer?" Our answer is an emphatic, "No!" it is called being a sales professional! It is recognizing the different styles of the customers and selling to them the way they prefer to buy. To understand why this is not manipulation, let's consider wise advice that has been passed along many generations:

*"Do unto others as **you** would have **them** do unto **you.**"*

You may remember this as "The Golden Rule," and it is a great rule to live by. We believe in it 110%, especially when it comes to honesty, values, ethics and consideration for the needs of others. However, with interpersonal communication, it can backfire because others may not wish to be treated the same way you like to be treated. Not every person buys the way you sell! The Golden Rule is salesperson-centric instead of the word Tony Alessandra coined known as the "The Platinum Rule," which states:

*"Do unto others as **they** would have **you** do unto **them**."*

When people are treated the way they want to be treated, you are paying attention to their needs, wants and expectations. You are trying to "walk a mile in their moccasins" and understand their feelings, see their point of view and identify their purchasing requirements. That builds trust, friendship and respect ... three requirements for any strong relationship.

When you understand your own style and how it differs from the styles of others, you can adapt your selling approach accordingly. Your ideas do not have to change, you just need to change the way you present them to the customer. This is called adaptability.

Adaptability is simply changing your behavior, not your personality, values or beliefs. Adaptable people consciously decide to modify their behaviors to a particular person, situation, or event. Less adaptable people, on the other hand, respond in a more habitual manner, regardless of whether the response is likely to be appropriate or effective. Guess which one is the more successful salesperson?

Getting along with others is the universal key to success. Experience has taught us that the ability to build rapport with others was one characteristic highly successful people have in common. The $uccessful Hotel $ales in 5 Easy $teps book provides the added bonus of cultivating successful relationships in all areas of your life…beyond a successful career in sales.

While it may be true that more and more of the sales function is performed with software platforms, like Cvent (a leading event management technology company) that make it easy to respond to a Request for Proposal (RFP), this book will give hotel salespeople a powerful tool to help them build rapport with customers, colleagues and quite possibly friends and family. We have based our model on years of research and validation; yet it is simple, practical, and easy to use and remember. It does not require salespeople to have customers take a personality test; it is a manner of strategically observing customer behaviors. Though this book was written with hotel salespeople in mind, it is an excellent resource for event and meeting planners who work the meetings, incentives, conferences, and exhibitions (MICE) market, too!

Please note the Appendix provides some additional resource materials for hotel salespeople. There are worksheets that can be filled out to master the materials presented in this book to guide future sales efforts. There are also summary tables on adapting to the fours styles that can be reviewed for a quick refresher when preparing to meet with a prospective client.

••••••••

This Book Is Broken Down Into Four Key Sections.

Section I describes the four general behavioral styles of your customers, helping salespeople to understand their own behavior style and know what type of sales position best matches their natural behaviors.

Section II describes the two basic behavioral dimensions and provides a simple process of elimination to help you identify yours and your customers' behavioral styles. It will also give you some scenarios on how to identify the four styles during a sales transaction.

Section III describes how to adapt your way of selling to the four styles. This requires behavioral adaptability on your part, so you can easily connect with those who have styles that are different from your own. You will not learn ways to manipulate others; you will learn skills that anyone working in sales should possess in order to identify and satisfy the needs of others to help them grow their business… and yours.

Section IV teaches you the five easy selling steps and how to build on each step to help each buyer identify and satisfy their needs. The five easy steps to sales success are Connecting, Exploring, Collaborating, Confirming, and Assuring.

Those who get the most out of the sales process described in this book have common characteristics, regardless of their behavioral style. They are confident in their ability as a hotel salesperson and trust their own judgement and resourcefulness. They are tolerant of others and possess an open-minded state of acceptance of others without judgment. They are empathetic and sensitive to the viewpoints of others and wise to adapt their selling style to that of customers. They have a positive attitude about people and do not dwell on losing an important piece of business to a competitor; instead they learn from their mistakes and do better job with the next opportunity to make a sale. They respect and understand that others have the right to live life as they see fit and do not let the personal choices of others interfere with a day in the office or out on a call. Even though they may be highly competitive, they can find a way to achieve win-win results. Most important of all, they are approachable and do not have to be reminded that they are in the hospitality business. They, like everyone else in the sales office, are there to provide high quality service to any and all of the hotel's prospective customers, no matter the size or scope of the potential piece of business. If this sounds like you, the $uccessful Hotel $ales in 5 Easy $teps book will deliver results in your sales efforts. It is not only a better way to sell all the services your hotel offers the marketplace ... *it's a better way to live!*

CHAPTER 1

HOTEL SALES 101: THE FIVE PRIMARY SELLING SKILLS

The question about which skills contribute to successful salespeople is not one that can be answered with a single attribute, but a combination of many with varying importance. Ask any hotel Director of Sales (DOS) and he/she will tell you: some skills can be taught and some cannot. Selling skills, like mathematics or social studies, can be taught if one has the aptitude for it. Attitude is almost impossible to teach. You either come to your job each day with a good attitude or you don't. When hiring salespeople, it is easy to look over a résumé and determine if a candidate has the right work experience to be qualified for an open position. The true test is to determine what type of attitude is possessed towards work, learning skills, accepting change, and more. A positive, proactive attitude can be seen in a number of ways. From the simplest of initial greetings to how he/she manages the overall sales process are clear indications of one's attitude.

Do you want to work with someone who comes in the office in the morning, goes into their office and never even says hello to teammates? Or, do you want to work with someone who comes into the office with a smile and an energetic "Good morning!" each day?

Do you want to work with someone who is looking for reasons why something will not work to increase sales? Or, do you want to work with someone who is always looking for ways to solve problems and meet or exceed sales goals and energizing the sales team in the process?

Do you want to work with someone who is constantly complaining about the way management is operating the hotel? Or do you want to work with someone who spends time looking for ways to make improvements?

The answers to those questions should be obvious. Most of us would prefer to work with salespeople who have a positive attitude!

In addition to attitude, there are five primary selling skills that are common among top hotel salespeople. They are **listening, prospecting, probing, communication** and **closing**. Each will be discussed in more detail below.

Of the five, the ability to be a good listener is the most important to those reading this book! The ability to sell <u>anything</u> is about **listening** to the customer to get a clear understanding of what is needed and then determining if your property meets their needs. Without the ability to listen, all you can do is ramble on about the features and benefits of your hotel rather than helping the customer realize they should choose your hotel over the competition.

Good **prospecting** skills are important when you are in a market where the business is not coming to you – You need to go out and get it. It takes a certain type of individual who is willing to pick up a telephone or walk into an office where he/she may be unwelcomed. The goal for these types of calls is to determine if the customer has needs that your property can satisfy. Good prospecting skills are an important factor in how successful you will be in getting business for your property.

Good **probing** techniques are another important part in determining whether you will be able to uncover the needs of your potential client. Understanding that people like to do business with people whom they have established a relationship; your probing skills will allow you to adapt the way you sell to match the way the customer prefers to buy, which will be explained in section III and IV of this book. You do not want to be perceived as just asking customers many questions and writing down their answers. You want to be able to get the information from the customer during the course of a pleasant business conversation in order to uncover their needs and wants and earn you the piece of business!

Communication skills are all encompassing. They include verbal, written, and presentation skills. Good salespeople know how to effectively communicate the ways in which their hotel will satisfy the needs and wants of customers. Your written communications skills are tested when you need to prepare a creative proposal to present to a client as well as when the Director of Sales asks you to write a memo justifying a prospecting trip you want to take to call on prospective customers.

Your verbal communication skills are tested every day. Your General Manager may want you to explain the reason you booked a particular piece of business over certain dates. Your Director of Sales might want you to make a verbal presentation to the Revenue Management Committee to explain the reason group rates for a particular time period were set so low. The ability to express your thoughts to others is most often tested through your verbal communication skills

Your presentation skills are a combination of your written, verbal, and personal presentation skills. You may be presenting your property to the Executive Committee of an Association as the desired site for their annual convention. You will have to present each of them with a copy of your written proposal. They will also expect some sort of visual presentation about the features and benefits of your property. Of course, you will need to be able to speak to them in a manner that makes them believe that your hotel will be able to exceed their expectations. The salesperson with the best presentation skills has a better chance of getting the business than the hotel salesperson that does a marginal job in presenting the property.

Closing skills are often some of the most difficult skills to master. Many salespeople are simply reluctant to take that final step and ask someone for his/her business. But what you will learn after reading this book is that closing will be a foregone conclusion if you follow the five easy step selling process described in this book.

Of course, the five primary selling skills are useless to hotel salespeople who do not have a positive **ATTITUDE!** A positive attitude goes a long way to sustaining the energy and enthusiasm it takes to be a successful hotel salesperson, when following the five step selling process described in this book!

THE EVOLUTION OF SALES

In a special report by the Hotel Sales Marketing Association International (HSMAI), Lalia Rach, Ed.D, made it clear that salespeople today must utilize a progressive development process to maintain skills and abilities necessary for success. Personally, salespeople must build new technical and behavioral skills. With regard to the business, salespeople must be able to shift to strategic thinking and improving their ability to add value where expected by the customer. These skills require the ability to plan and build strategy.

More importantly, the way in which the five primary selling skills have been used by salespeople has evolved over time, as shown in Table 1. Salespeople in the 1800s took the approach of making a sale at any cost compared to today where they are more of a problem-solver. The salesperson used to hold all the power when negotiating a sale. These days the Internet allows buyers to have as much information, if not more, than the salesperson; so more power than before to negotiate a better deal for themselves. The role of the buyer has also changed to one that affords mutual benefits to the seller over a longer period of time. Although the bait and switch sales technique is still used by some salespeople these days, more often than not astute salespeople will use a team approach to solving the buyer's needs. Of course, lumping all salespeople into the category of "used car salesperson" persisted into the late 1960s but that perception is changing as more salespeople learn to adapt to the needs and wants of the buyer during sales transactions. But more than that, this book will teach you how to match the way you sell with the way the customer buys, through adaptability, a key skill that makes our easy the five step selling process such a powerful sales tool for hotel salespeople.

TABLE 1: EVOLUTION OF SELLING METHODS*

	Manupulation	Control	Consultation	Collaboration
Timeframe	1800s to 1920s	1920s to late 1960s	Late 1960s to late 1990s	Late 1990s to present
Primary Approach	Make the sale through any means even if premise is unethical, illegal or untrue	Father knows best, knowledge controlled by seller, to create needs	Identify prospect/ buyer needs; connect to benefits of product/ service	Solve problems; provide advice; work together
Power	Seller	Seller	Seller	Buyer
Role of Prospect or Buyer	Sporadic occurrences; emotionally based	Standardized interactions utilizing phone, conventions, drop-by, scheduled meetings, ads	Salesperson as expert creating win-win situation for individual client	Complex exchange of advice, solutions, ideas. Mutual benefit, long-term.
Relationship	Sporadic occurrences; emotionally based	Standardized interactions utilizing phone, conventions, drop-by, scheduled meetings, ads	Salesperson as expert creating win-win situation for individual client	Complex exchange of advice, solutions, ideas. Mutual benefit, long-term.
Sales Technique	Bait and switch; pressure (peer, status)	Product/ service is the best way to solve the buyer's problems. Hunters and gathers.	Someone buyer likes to do business with	Integrated team approach to solving buyer problems. Planning and analysis.
Descriptors	Snake oil salesman, used car salesman	Schmooze, wine and dine, charisma	Expert advice from a trusted source	Insight, buyer oriented

*NOTE: (Adapted from Finkelstein, in HSMAI Special Report on the Evolution of Sales)

SECTION I

THE FOUR BEHAVIORAL STYLES

For some of you, the "4 styles" model of human behavior is a new concept. However, many of you have probably encountered this concept in high school or your psychology classes in college. "Behavioral styles," "personality types" and "temperament types" are not new; they all have validity. What makes The Platinum Rule different from the rest of the psychological profiles is that it is based on observable behaviors, NOT "personalities" or "temperaments." This distinction is critical because people behave in ways that are consistent with their behavioral style. When you learn to adapt to the behavioral cues that you are observing, you will gain rapport with that customer. You are not adapting to their "personality;" you are identifying their "behavioral style" which is more stable over time.

What will you be observing? Whether you know it or not, the way people act, how they are dressed, the pace at which they talk, their occupation, their desire to be the center of attention (or not), their job title, and the way their office is decorated are tangible cues that indicate a person's style. There is no mundane checklist to use to sell an event; it is time to adapt the list to the style of the customer!

Before we get started! One of the things we highly recommend when reading the description of the four behavioral styles in Section I is to identify someone in your life who epitomizes each style. It may be a key customer, your spouse, your neighbor, your golfing partner, or a vendor.

In doing so, you will realize what makes those people different – based on their behavioral style – and better understand why they behave the way they do. Once you learn to recognize the styles of those you know best, you will be equipped to read the style of the next customer who walks into the hotel to book a piece of business or when making a sales call to reach out to prospective or current customers.

CHAPTER 2

DIRECTORS:
THE GREAT INITIATORS

Directors initiate change, momentum, and growth. They focus on attaining their goals; their key need is to achieve their bottom-line results. The driving need for results, combined with their motto of "Lead, follow, or get out of the way," explains their no-nonsense, direct approach to accomplish their goals.

Directors are driven by an inner need to be in personal control. They want to take charge of situations so they can be sure of goals attainment.

DIRECTORS NEED ACHIEVEMENT AND CONTROL

Directors want to win so they may naturally challenge people or practices in the process. They accept challenges, take authority, and plunge into solving problems. They tend to focus on administrative and operational controls and can work quickly and impressively by themselves.

Directors are naturals at being in control. They tend to be independent, strong-willed, precise, goal-oriented, and competitive with others, especially in a business environment. They try to shape their environment in order to overcome obstacles en route to their accomplishments. They demand freedom to manage themselves and others, using their drive to become winners. They start, juggle and maintain many projects concurrently. They may continue to add projects to their juggling routine until they are overloaded and then drop everything, calling it a "re-evaluation of their priorities." After reducing their workload, and stress levels, they often immediately start the whole process again. Their motivation pattern contributes to a Director's tendency to be a "workaholic."

Primary skills include the ability to get things done, lead others, and make decisions. They are able to focus on one task at the Director's exclusion of everything else. They can ignore doorbells, sirens, or other people while channeling their energies into the specific job at hand.

ON THE OTHER HAND...

With each of the four behavioral styles, negative traits may accompany many of the positive attributes. Any characteristic has a dark side when taken to an extreme. For Directors, some negative traits may include stubbornness, impatience, and an appearance of toughness. Directors tend to take control of other people and can have a low tolerance for the feelings, attitudes, and shortcomings among co-workers and subordinates. They may annoy others because their constant need to be come out on top and "always be right" can be offensive. The saying "there's more than one way to skin a cat" does not apply to the Director; there is only one way – the way the Director would do it!

Directors like to move at a fast pace and tend to become impatient with delays. It is not unusual for a Director to call someone and launch into a conversation without saying "Hello." Oftentimes, Directors tend to view others who move at a slower speed as less competent. Their weaknesses tend to include impatience, intolerance, poor listening habits, and insensitivity to the needs of others. Their complete focus on their own goals and immediate tasks may make them appear aloof and uncaring.

In addition, Directors hold one to the terms and agreement of the sale. However, the same rules may not apply to them, because if the agreement of the sale becomes inconvenient for them they will attempt to have you bend the rules to accommodate their needs. If this happens, concessions should be offered (giving in will be seen as weakness) and one should be prepared to defend the decision to abide by the original agreement. If one concedes to a Director, it is important to get a concession in return or offer to negotiate new terms and agreements with future sales. Earning respect with Directors will ensure a positive long-term relationship.

DIRECTORS ARE DECISIVE

Directors embrace challenges, take authority, make decisions quickly, and expect others to do the same. They prefer to work with people who are decisive, efficient, receptive, competent, and intelligent. You may often find Directors in top management positions; their personal strengths often contribute to their success in jobs such as a hard-driving reporter, a stockbroker, an independent consultant, or a drill sergeant! Under pressure, Directors often vent their anger by ranting, raving, or challenging others. While relieving their own inner tensions, they often create stress and tension for others.

"WINNING ISN'T EVERYTHING..."

The competitive nature of the Director is captured by Vince Lombardi's now-famous statement that, "Winning isn't everything... it's the only thing!" Directors can be so single-minded that they forget to celebrate their victories as they move on to the next conquest.

DIRECTORS AT A GLANCE:

Needs to be in charge; dislike inaction	Acts quickly and decisively
Thinks practically, not theoretically or hypothetically	Wants highlighted facts
Competes at a high level	Needs personal freedom to manage self and others
Likes change and new opportunities	Prefers to delegate details
Likes to be independent	Has a low tolerance for feelings of others
Works quickly and impressively alone	Wants to be recognized for their accomplishments
Wants to win at all costs (second place is first loser)	Enjoys arguments and conflict

THE SOCIAL SCENE WITH DIRECTORS

Directors tend to take charge in social settings... sometimes inappropriately. Their relationships would improve if they would demonstrate respect for other people's rights and opinions, allowing others to take charge… while "letting go." Directors have trouble having fun for fun's sake and usually have a specific purpose in mind. The competitive Director has a tendency to try to win even in relaxed social settings. The Director is always conscious of his standing in the "biggest and best" games and difficult to outmatch. "Who has the biggest house?" "Who gives the best parties?" "Who plays the best golf?" If your house is 3,000 square feet, theirs is 4,000. If you bought a new suit made of Italian wool for $2,000, they got a better deal for $1,500.

Directors often intertwine business and friendships. They like to mix their own business interests with pleasure so they choose friends from their work pool. Friendships often hinge on how much the friend agrees with the Director and helps him achieve his goals. Potential friendships are like an experiment with the Director: If it works, fine. If not, goodbye!

Director humor can be biting, often directed at others. They tend to take themselves too seriously and could benefit from learning to relax, laugh more, and enjoy the lighter side of their own—and others'—actions.

Typical social behaviors of Directors may include:

- Competing actively in almost everything

- Participating in games or contests to win

- Wanting to know the purpose of a function

- Talking shop at social gatherings

Preferred social situations for Directors:

- Having many options from which to choose, for example: either jogging, attending an event, dining out, or playing cards

- Paying more attention to tactile things but less to emotions

- Doing only what they prefer to do

- Occasions that favor direct humor with an opportunity to demonstrate their talents

- Having a group subject to their control

- Being in charge of some function at social events and activities (e.g. judging, giving directions, chairing a fund-raiser)

DIRECTORS STYLE AT WORK

Directors can be excellent problem solvers and leaders. Higher power positions and/or career areas motivate them so you will often find them in leadership positions. Directors are more formal and prefer to maintain their physical and psychological distance from others. They are sensitive about personal space and do not like to have people get too close.

The typical office arrangement is formal with seating that is face-to-face with a big "power desk" separating the Director from his visitors. A Director's desk is likely to be busy with paperwork, projects and material separated into organized piles. Both in-baskets and out-baskets typically bulge with paperwork. Directors also tend to be surrounded by trophies, awards, and other evidence of personal achievement. Everything about their office signals hustle, bustle, formality, and power.

Director's preferred power decoration generally includes a large chair behind a massive desk, providing separation from visitors. The walls of their office display plaques, degrees, awards, and other evidence of success as well as large event calendars or project tracking charts. Any photos will probably be with dignitaries or celebrities that communicate a high level of status or importance. If family photos are displayed, they are usually placed behind the Director, not to be distracted from the business at hand. You might even find inspirational sayings such as, "If I do not find the road to success, I will build it myself!"

You will often find Directors in the following types of positions:

- President, CEO, or the formally recognized leader

- Politician

- Law enforcement officer

- Military officer

- Executive

- Hotel General Manager

- Stock Broker

- General contractor

- Coach

A typical Director sees himself as a solutions-oriented manager who enjoys a challenge "because it's there." He likes the opportunity to complete tasks in a creative manner. He is generally viewed as having a high level of confidence, even when it is not necessarily the case. The Director is often the first person to arrive in the morning and the last person to leave in the evening. At the extreme, his/her high results orientation can lead to an overextended work pattern and result in neglect for personal and social lives.

Directors are the first person at work to have a new status "toy": the faster computer or the newest smartphone. Saving time is always a priority for Directors so more can be accomplished.

Directors gain energy by taking risks, feeling less bound by conventional restrictions as other types and often feeling free to bend rules that get in the way of results. They seek opportunities for change or create them to satisfy their need for results. They may even gravitate toward high-risk situations because the excitement of the challenge fuels their drive to exert control in new areas or ways.

Directors realize that results can be gained through teamwork and may actually develop a management approach that demands and supports teamwork, but it requires adaptation. The nature of the Director is to focus on his own individual actions and accomplishments. In his biography, Lee Iacocca, former CEO of Chrysler Corporation (a "Director legend"), discusses how he learned to merge his temperament with other styles as he finally arrived at the following management philosophy: "In the end, all business operations can be reduced to three words: people, products, profits. People come first. Unless you have a good team, you can't do much with the other two." Iacocca knew that good people were the means to an end.

Director business characteristics include:

- Prefers controlled timeframes

- Seeks personal control

- Gets to the point quickly

- Strives to feel important and be noteworthy on their job

- Demonstrates persistence and single-mindedness in reaching goals

- Expresses high ego need

- Prefers to downplay feelings and relationships

- Focuses on task actions that lead to achieving tangible outcomes

- Implements changes in the workplace

- Tends to freely delegate duties in order to take on more tasks and pursue more goals

Preferred business situations for Directors:

- Calling the shots and telling others what to do

- Challenging workloads to fuel energy levels

- Personally overseeing, or knowing about, employees' or co-workers' business activities

- Saying what is on their mind without concern about hurting anyone's feelings

- Taking risks and being involved in facilitating changes

- Interested in the answers to "what" questions

- Seeing a logical road toward advancement of achieving goals

DIRECTOR SALESPEOPLE

The natural tendency of the Director salesperson is to launch rather quickly into a sales presentation. They get right to the point by telling your customer the bottom-line benefit of using your property to accomplish the goals and objectives of your event meeting. Their natural tendency is to spend little time chatting or getting to know your customers… unless it is required to get the sale! Directors move quickly, and if a customer does not see the benefit of their proposal, they move on to the next prospective customer.

Directors have a fast, efficient manner and total focus on goals that make them more comfortable than most people with cold calling. They are able to tolerate negatives as a necessary part of the sales process. Their bottom-line orientation fits their focus on products or services, which adds efficiency to their customer acquisition processes. Directors tend to sell by painting a convincing picture of the benefits of their product or service.

Be careful when implementing sales contests to stimulate sales due to the highly competitive nature of the Director. The Director will step over the bodies of the sales team members to "win at all costs" to collect the first place prize that goes to the winner.

Directors perform best when the existing features and benefits of the property match up perfectly with the needs and expectations of the customer. Meetings and events that require lengthy tailoring, customization and/or development try their patience. They prefer sales processes where quick decisions can be made based on rational, concrete, reality-based data.

Director salespeople are very careful about time, especially their own! They tend to make specific time appointments and arrive punctually. They are clear about their desired results from customer contacts and quickly present the features and benefits offered by their product or service.

Director's Emails, Letters and Memos

Directors correspondence tend to be brief and to the point. Directors may mention highlights of conversations or materials but leave out the details unless required to do so. They generally include specifics for your follow-through or raise questions needing to be answered now! Even notes and cards take on abbreviated forms and with little or no strong feelings and/or tone expressed.

On the Phone with a Director

Again, Directors prefer to be brief and get right to the point, especially when it is their time or your agenda! They may start the conversation with whatever task they are focused on with no personal acknowledgement or greeting. They often speak in shorthand and get right to the point while sounding cool, confident, and demanding. Phone calls sometimes sound like human telegrams, tending to speak loudly, rapidly, and emphatically. Lacking good active listening skills, one may get the sense that they are not being listened to. However, one must be careful what he/she says to Directors as they may replay the conversation later in their head. Upon reflection, if something seemed amiss about what was said, it could shake their confidence and the sale will be lost.

THE DIRECTOR CUSTOMER

Director customers will make decisions relatively quickly when presented with factual information. They want to see the bottom-line impact of how your property will help them accomplish the goals and objectives with enough detail to indicate you are competent to handle their business. Directors are generally businesslike, straightforward, and to-the-point while preferring others to do the same. They expect their goals and concerns to be taken seriously. They respect salespeople who offer them solutions to their problems in a professional manner and expect salespeople to deliver the results that were promised.

What the Director customers want to know is how your property will solve their problems most effectively right now. Directors are not natural listeners; details and lengthy explanations are likely to be lost during the presentation. Salespeople are expected to provide useful information immediately and make recommendations that will move Directors toward their goals. Be careful when answering the detailed questions of Directors; more than anything else they are designed to determine if the salesperson is competent to handle the business. If a Director does request additional detailed information about a proposal it should be done in writing so he/she can scrutinize it later.

Director customers look for solutions that will help them achieve their goals. They maintain control of the sales process and prefer salespeople who provide the information and data necessary to make a sound decision. They are competitive and respond well to products or services that are "the best."

Directors expect results now and are impatient with waiting. They expect salespeople to respond to impossible deadlines even if it means sacrificing personal time. They are not especially interested in developing relationships with the salesperson, but it is important for them to believe that the salesperson can help them get desired results. They like being recognized for their achievements, responding well to awards banquets, "special customer" celebrations, and other recognitions that acknowledge their involvement in the buying/selling process.

Time is an important factor for goal-oriented Directors. They do not tolerate having salespeople waste their time and do not want to waste that of others. This includes time spent on small talk. Directors are more comfortable as a team leader than as a team player. As a result, they tend to make decisions without the involvement of others.

Directors like to have choices, have options, and exercise their decision-making power. Each possible solution to their business need should be a reasonable choice backed by evidence supporting its probability of success. Such buyers have clear objectives to achieve and respond to those who can demonstrate that their property will competently handle their piece of business over the competition.

UPON REFLECTION

Do you know a Director? Is it your boss, the one who always wants to be in control or one up's everybody no matter the topic of conversation? Is it your spouse who just cannot seem to keep his or her mind off work? Is it the youth soccer coach who is treating the kids like they are paid professionals and focusing on winning over simply enjoying how to learn to play soccer? Is the line "There is no crying in baseball," (uttered by Tom Hanks, from the movie a *League of their Own*), one of your bosses favorite movie quotes? Do they tend to be the customers who always feel like you are not giving them the best deal and looking for proof that they are right? If you know people who have these behaviors, chances are you now know a Director or two. Moreover, when selling to this style, it is not a simple negotiation; it is a battle of wills!

CHAPTER 3

SOCIALIZERS:
THE GREAT TALKERS

Socializers are stimulating, talkative, friendly, enthusiastic, and like to be part of the social scene. They thrive on admiration, acknowledgement, compliments and applause. They want to have fun and enjoy life. Energetic and fast-paced, Socializers tend to place more priority on relationships than on tasks. They influence others by their optimistic, friendly demeanor and they focus primarily on attaining positive approval from others.

SOCIALIZERS NEED ATTENTION AND APPROVAL

Admiration and acceptance are extremely important to Socializers. Often, they are not as concerned about winning or losing as how they look while they are "playing the game." The Socializer's greatest fear is public humiliation: appearing uninvolved, unattractive, unsuccessful, or unacceptable to others. These frightening forms of social rejection threaten the Socializer's core need for approval. As a result, when conflict occurs, Socializers may abruptly take flight for more favorable environments.

The Socializers' primary strengths are their enthusiasm, persuasiveness, and friendliness. They are "idea-a-minute" people who have the ability to get others caught up in their dreams. With great persuasion, they shape their environments by building personal alliances to accomplish results. Then they seek comments of approval and recognition for those results. If compliments do not come, Socializers may invent their own!

Socializers are generally open with their ideas and feelings but sometimes only at superficial levels. They feel compelled to share their personal thoughts and stories whether you asked for them to or not. They are animated, interactive storytellers who have no qualms about creative exaggeration. They love an audience and thrive on involvement with people, working quickly and enthusiastically with others. They are risk takers and base many of their actions and decisions on natural impulse and feelings. Their greatest irritations are doing repetitive or complex tasks, being alone, or not having access to a telephone!

ON THE OTHER HAND...

Socializer's weaknesses are too much involvement in too many projects, impatience, aversion to being alone, and short attention spans. They become bored quickly and easily. They often make sweeping generalizations when a little data is evident. When Socializers feel they do not have enough stimulation and involvement, they get bored and look for something new... repeatedly. They are also impulse shoppers you will see in line at the supermarket fidgeting with last minute items on display, or checking out what others in line have bought, awaiting their turn to check out.

When taken to an extreme, Socializer behaviors may appear superficial, haphazard, erratic, and overly emotional. Their need for acknowledgement can lead to self-absorption. They have a casual approach to time and often drive the other styles "crazy" with their missed deadlines and lateness. Fun loving, life-of-the-party Socializers can be undisciplined, forgetful, overly talkative, and too eager for credit and recognition. Their natural humor often bubbles over even in serious situations, which should have called for more reserved behavior. More often than not, if someone is going to say something inappropriate, no matter the social setting, it is likely to be the Socializer!

It is likely that those working in hotel sales are Socializers. How do we know? Dr La Lopa has administered the Behavioral Styles Questionnaire to thousands of hospitality students at Purdue University in West Lafayette, Indiana and 55% test out as Socializers.

Socializers are likely to be public relations specialists, talk show hosts, motivational speakers, trial attorneys, social directors on cruise ships, and other people-intensive positions in profit and nonprofit organizations.

Audience reactions stimulate Socializers they thrive in entertainment fields where their natural, animated actions can flow easily. They like to charm friends, co-workers, and audiences with their friendliness and enthusiasm.

You probably know some Socializers in your family, at the office, or at home. They always have something to say. They are the people you ask, "How is it going?" and twenty minutes later, they are still talking your ear off. It may come as no surprise that their most favorite thing to talk about is … themselves! Almost to the point of telling others, "Hey, I am tired of talking about myself, why don't you talk about me for a while."

SOCIALIZERS AT A GLANCE:

Crave interaction and human contact	Act with enthusiasm and expression
Act and decide spontaneously	Concerned with approval and appearances
Make decisions based on emotions	Think of the "big picture" and bored with details
Like change and innovation	Need help getting and staying organized
Dislike conflict	Maintain a positive, optimistic orientation about life
Exaggerate and generalize	Dream aloud, get others caught up in their dreams
Jump from one activity to another	Work quickly and excitedly with others
Tells more about self than one cares to know	Like to exercise their persuasive skills

THE SOCIAL SCENE WITH THE SOCIALIZER

Socializers love being around people. Their lives are an open book; they are likely to discuss most subjects, no matter how close or distant your relationship. Showing and sharing their feelings come naturally to this behavioral type. Of the four styles, Socializers are the most comfortable talking about personal topics: marriage, finances, politics, aspirations, and problems. They digress from topic to topic and activity to activity, often leaving their listeners bewildered.

Socializers revel in humor (even if directed at them) and often tell hair-raising anecdotes about their experiences. The wilder the situation the better; even a little embellishment only make their stories sound that much more exciting and entertaining. They love to talk; telling a story better and funnier than it actually happened comes naturally to them.

Such a tendency to talk and tell stories can be a problem when privacy or confidences are involved. A Socializer naturally considers all conversations to be open. Unless they are expressly told not to tell anyone about the topic, they are not likely to realize the importance of keeping some information confidential.

Socializers are naturally optimistic and ready with an encouraging pep talk when the people around them are unhappy or have problems. They praise and support others, in part, in order to create a positive environment where they can satisfy their own needs for social approval. Compliments and encouragement make them feel good, even when the praise is directed at someone else!

Socializers like to be the life of the party. You will often find them in the middle of a circle of admirers. Their willingness to discuss any topic often invites controversy and they love a lively debate. They gain energy from the dynamics of relationships and talking; they despise feeling bored. People rally around them because they know how to create fun and find (or make) the action. They are playful and enjoy companionship; they hate isolation.

Of the four types, Socializers really want to be liked by others. They will monitor the body language, vocal inflections, and eye contact of others to make sure they are being viewed in a favorable light. Should they detect that they have fallen out of favor among those they are entertaining, they will work even harder to win back the approval of others. It hurts their feelings when disliked by others; even the slightest criticism can be deflating.

Socializers are notorious for being "fashionably late." People may think they are trying to make a grand entrance, but their lateness generally results from their casual approach and resulting miscalculations about time. They often forget details of social obligations and get so caught up in what they are presently doing that they lose track of time and place. If you want the Socializer to be on time, tell them the party starts one hour earlier than you tell everyone else to show up!

Typical social behavior of Socializer:

- Wants to be liked and admired

- Fears public humiliation

- Discusses most subjects, regardless of how distant or casual the relationship

- Feels warmth and enthusiasm

- Enjoys bouncing ideas off others

- Avoids fights or confrontation with people or situations

- Perceives life according to feelings

- Discusses emotions with others

- Chooses associates and friends by "gut instinct" and trial-and-error

Preferred social situations of Socializers:

- Personal interaction and contact through events and activities

- Host or attend impromptu gatherings

- Enjoy fun people with different interests

- Seek more positive people and settings

- Find it easy to laugh, joke, and play games

- Seeks high-visibility positions (e.g., storyteller, emcee)

- Prefer humor that pokes fun at their own and others' foibles

- Try to diffuse mild tension with jokes or amusing observations

- Prefer to ignore sources of stress (e.g., conflict, complex tasks)

- Like to share the moment with others

SOCIALIZERS STYLE AT WORK

Socializers prefer careers that maximize their influence and persuasion with other people. They tend to gravitate to environments that allow them to socialize, mingle, and gain positive feedback. They also tend to interrupt the work of others because they need to share what is going on in their head with others.

Socializers respond to visual stimuli; they like to have everything where they can see it. Consequently, their desks often look cluttered and disorganized and they may even pile paperwork and files across their desk or on the floor. A favorite motto of Socializers (usually taped to an almost buried in-basket) reads: "A Clean Desk is the Sign of a Sick Mind."

Socializer's walls usually display awards and displays of their current interests. These might include motivational or upbeat slogans or posters, cartoons, drawings, or quotations. You may see reminder notes posted all over the place with little apparent forethought, rhyme, or reason. Socializers, if asked, will take great pride to explain to you all the things that are on their desk or on the wall because it gives them a chance to talk about themselves and their interests.

Typically, the preferred decor of the Socializer office would be an open, airy, lively atmosphere that represents the personality of its occupant. The furniture arrangement serves as an open invitation for visitors to feel welcomed. Socializers do not like barriers such as a desk to be separate from others. Comfortable, accessible seating is preferred to be able to get to know others. Socializers talk a lot, with their emotional nature shown in both body language and speech. Since Socializers are touchers and do not mind a slap on the back or a warm handshake, they often use an alternative seating arrangement to get physically closer to visitors. There is little danger of alienating Socializers by standing too close or picking up something from their desks.

Socializers often work in these types of careers:

- Customer relations

- Public relations

- Being on stage entertaining, acting, singing, reporting, public speaking, etc.

- Professional host or emcee

- Hospitality (e.g., hotel sales, server, bartender)

- Motivational Speaker

- Politician

- Salesperson

- Teacher

Socializers are happy working with other people. They like being treated with warmth, friendliness, and approval. Because they favor interacting with people on more than only a business level, they want to be your friend before doing business with you.

Socializers like a quick pace and often move about the office in a flurry of activity. They even walk in a way that reflects optimism and pace ... lively and energetically. They tend to think aloud and often walk around the office talking to almost everyone. While this may appear to be "goofing off" to more Director-style managers, Socializers pick up much of their information by talking to others and observing their surroundings. They are likely to brainstorm about matters with virtually everyone they encounter. It is important for them to find out how other people feel about their ideas. They also like feedback and occasional positive reinforcement that these impromptu encounters provide. They enjoy a casual, relaxed environment where their impulses can have free rein. Desk hopping also satisfies their need for companionship. They like to play and mingle as they learn, earn, and do practically everything else.

Since Socializers are naturally talkative and people-oriented, dealing with people who are in positions of power meets their need for inclusion by others, popularity, and social recognition. Socializers are good at getting others caught up in their ideas. Their persuasive powers may simultaneously amaze admirers and frustrate detractors. These smooth-talking tendencies can be perceived as silver-tongued oration or evasive double-talk. Socializers may appear to be a verbal Pied Piper, or even a wheeling and dealing con artist.

Socializers want companionship and social recognition; their contributions to group morale often satisfy those needs. They encourage their employees, peers, and superiors to excel. They typically look outside themselves to renew their energies and enjoy motivational books, tapes, and speeches. They need these pick-me-ups to recharge their batteries and help them overcome obstacles. Their typically optimistic outlook changes problems into challenges or opportunities.

The Big Picture is much more interesting to Socializers than the details. After seeing the broad overview, they prefer not to personally dwell on specifics. Their enthusiasm helps them generate many ideas and their tendency to get feedback from everyone around them helps select ideas that have a good chance to be fruitful.

Socializer's tend to dominate conversations with others, regardless of the situation. They are naturally impulsive; sometimes their spontaneous behavior is energizing, but sometimes it is frustrating. They continually seek new ideas. Sometimes this is irritating to the people around them who think that a solution has been settled upon… only to have Socializers start a new round of potential solutions. While others think Socializers were committed to something, they were merely thinking aloud. That is why Socializers are much better at generating ideas than implementing them.

Socializers do not respond well to authoritative or dictatorial management styles, often possessed and displayed by the Director, especially under stress or tight deadlines. The boss that orders the Socializer to do one thing may receive just the opposite. Socializers may get defensive and become less willing to cooperate. On the other hand, the boss that chooses to take the time to inspire the Socializer to accomplish a goal will find it hard to find a more dedicated, committed, hard worker.

This is particularly true once Socializers have had time to "connect" the significance of the work to their dreams, their financial future, or their opportunity to be publically acknowledged for their accomplishments.

Socializer business characteristics:

- Like to brainstorm and interact with colleagues and others

- Want freedom from control, details, or complexity

- Like to have the chance to influence, persuade or motivate others

- Like being a key part of an exciting team

- Want to be included by others in important projects, activities or events

- Get easily bored by routine and repetition

- May trust others without reservation; takes others at their word and does not check for themselves

- Typically have short attention spans, so they do better with frequent, short breaks

- Prefer talking to listening

Preferred business situations for Socializers:

- Work interactively with others

- Need personal feedback and discussion to get—or stay—on course

- Mingle with all levels of associates and calls them by their first names

- Enjoy compliments about themselves and their accomplishments

- Stimulating environments that are friendly and favorable

- Work on known, specific, quickly attainable incentives or external motivators (dislikes pursuits which drag out over long time periods)

- Open to verbal or demonstrated guidance for transferring ideas into action

- Like to start projects, but prefers to let others handle the follow-through and detail work

SOCIALIZER SALESPEOPLE

Socializer salespeople have a positive attitude, are enthusiastic, open-minded and have a natural inclination toward people. These attributes provide them with a head start in the sales process. Socializers are excellent at making contact, networking, and socializing. They thrive in a stimulating workplace. Their best sales situation gives them an opportunity to meet and greet many people, but it does not require a lengthy needs analysis or negotiation process.

Socializer salespeople like situations that give them a lot of freedom and provide variety and fun. They emphasize their appearance, wanting to look prosperous and successful. Socializers tend to have the newest cell phone, stylish clothes, and other status symbols that say, "Hey, look at me!"

They excel when the event they booked brings happiness to their customers. Even more so when the client acknowledges the role Socializers played in planning and managing a successful event.

With their creative minds and advanced communication skills, Socializers are great at painting mental pictures for customers. Using sentences that begin with, "Just imagine how glamorous the bride will look…" or "Your event will be remembered for years when…" are common. They tend to be the best of the four styles for generating a long list of corresponding benefits for every feature offered by a product or service they are selling.

Socializer salespeople are odd in some respects. Although they will take the time to know the customers' personal likes and dislikes, as well as readily share their own, they may forget their names, birthdays, where they attended college, and so forth. This is not because they do not care, (they have every intention of remembering and doing all these things), but once they move on to the next prospective customer, they often forget the fine details of the previous customer to better focus on the opportunity at hand.

Socializer's Emails, Letters and Memos

Look for exclamation points, underlining and bold highlighting in memos of Socializers. If it's an email, you might find unusual fonts, several colors and graphics, or emojis. In their text, you can almost hear Socializers emphasizing those emotion-laden, colorful adjectives and adverbs. Socializers write in the same stimulating, energetic way that they speak. If they take the time to write a letter, Socializers will include personal anecdotes or references to shared experiences. Socializers are famous for their postscripts and might even include a "P.P.S.: ____." You might also find that they will respond to e-mails without really reading them and you will be puzzled by their responses as nonsensical. So, you may need to encourage them to reread the e-mail you sent to get a coherent response.

On the Phone with Socializers

"What's up?" "What's happening?" or "How's it going?" are common opening lines for Socializers. Their animation and gestures emanate through the phone line as if they are in the room with you. Socializers love the phone and recharge their batteries by talking to others. They speak rapidly with a lot of emphasis and emotion; they can talk longer and better than the other styles. When calling from a poor mobile phone connection, they may talk for two or three minutes before they even realize the call was dropped. What they love most about phones is the ability to instantly connect anywhere, anytime with others.

SOCIALIZER CUSTOMERS

Socializer customers will make purchasing decisions quickly if they become excited by an opportunity placed before them. They dislike getting bogged down with a lot of details and data about the business they want to book, but will listen intently to the benefits. In fact, with their fast, creative minds, they often see the benefits long before you point them out. When this happens, compliment them for their quick thinking and their "big picture" vision, but otherwise… don't speak! At that moment, you are the second-best salesperson in the conversation – they will sell themselves.

Socializers base many of their decisions on intuition or first impressions. They need to be liked and admired; it helps if salespeople understand what makes them look good, both personally and professionally. They look for fun and creativity in the buying/selling process and respond well to invitations to social gatherings like lunches, golf outings, celebrations, and others. They prefer to know the personal likes and dislikes of salespeople, and vice-versa.

Socializers do not like bureaucracy or tedious paperwork. They want the sales process to be simple and easy… they want to say "yes" and then have everything magically happen without their further involvement. They are so positive and optimistic that they often expect more out of the piece of business that they booked than the hotel intended to deliver.

Socializers are "big picture" people who enjoy having many possibilities, but may then need help from the salesperson to narrow the choices and focus on one solution. And most of important of all, the salesperson must keep them aware of exactly how much their dream wedding is going to cost to keep them within their budget.

Once a decision is made, they tend to be very enthusiastic and cannot wait until they begin their stay at your hotel. So make sure that they get the proverbial "sizzle with the steak" or their disappointment in you and the hotel will be profound. They have a wide circle of friends and you can be sure they will share that disappointment with everyone they know costing you more business than you can imagine, especially given their love of social media.

Socializers will take risks when planning an event if convinced it will help move them closer to their dream. It is also important for them to know there is not a steep learning curve for planning and playing host to an event. If they suspect one, they may choose another hotel to book their event because the salespeople make planning simple and easy.

Be absolutely sure to take the time to review the terms and conditions of the contract before having Socializers sign it. Although it may make their head spin, it will be important to walk Socializers through the details of their event, including banquet event orders (BEO), so that they the hotel delivers the event that they are dreaming of in the way they had envisioned at the agreed price.

UPON REFLECTION

Stop and think for a moment. Do you know someone who is a Socializer? Perhaps it was that college teacher who was quite animated and told humorous stories to make learning fun. If in hotels sales, does it sound like you – or those you work with on a daily basis? Is it that co-worker who is always full of energy, singing songs out loud, giving cheerful hellos to everyone (even perfect strangers), and loves selling? Is it your neighbor who is always throwing backyard barbecues to entertain friends, family, or business associates? Perhaps it is that customer who has a hard time paying attention to the details when working on contract for an upcoming business meeting that must be fun and entertaining, rather than stuffy and boring. Such being the case, you have known a Socializer.

CHAPTER 4

THINKERS:
THE GREAT ANALYZERS

Thinkers are analytical, persistent, and systematic problem solvers. They are more concerned with logic and content than style. Thinkers prefer involvement with products and services under specific, controlled, predictable conditions so they can continue to perfect the performance, process, and results.

THINKERS SEEK ORDER AND ASSURANCES

The primary concern of Thinkers is accuracy; this means that emotions are less important. They believe feelings are more subjective and distort objectivity. Their biggest fear is of uncontrolled emotions and irrational acts, possibly preventing achievement of their objectives. They are uncomfortable with emotionality and/or irrationality in others. Thinkers strive to avoid embarrassment by attempting to control both themselves and their emotions. Of the four styles, Thinkers are the most risk-conscious and have a high need for accuracy. Combining these factors may lead them to an over-reliance on the collection of information and input from too many sources.

Thinkers prefer to deal with tasks rather than people and they like to have clearly defined priorities. They like to operate at a methodical pace, which also allows them to check and recheck their work. They tend to focus on the serious, more complicated aspects of situations. But when they are relaxed, their natural mental wit enables them to appreciate the lighter side of situations. They are often the first to see the bizarre nature or potential in situations.

Of the four styles, Thinkers are the most cerebrally oriented. They make decisions logically and cautiously to increase the probability that they will take the best available action. They are deliberate and strive to be technically perfect. Thinkers demand a lot from themselves and may succumb to overly critical tendencies. In general, they tend to keep their criticisms to themselves, hesitating to tell people what they think is deficient or incorrect. They typically share information, both positive and negative, only if requested or on a need-to-know basis and only if they have received assurances that there will be no negative consequences to them.

When Thinkers have definite, precise knowledge of facts and conditions, they quietly hold their ground. They can be indirectly assertive when they perceive they are in control of a relationship or their environment. After determining the specific risks, margins of error, and any other variables that significantly influence the desired results, they will take action. Often their actions may be subtle and indirect. However, if they can control the outcomes, their actions may be more swift and direct.

Thinkers' strengths include accuracy, independence, clarification and verification, fine-tuning and organization. They naturally focus on expectations (i.e.; policies, practices, and procedures), processes and outcomes. They want to know how things work so their own actions can be correct. Their core personal need is for autonomy in controlling the processes involved in fulfilling expectations in moving toward the intended outcomes.

Thinkers tend to be serious and orderly and are likely to be perfectionists. They tend to focus on the more critical details in the process of work and become irritated by surprises or glitches. They like organization and structure but dislike involvement with too many people or with any one person for too long of a period. They work meticulously by themselves and prefer objective, task-oriented, intellectual work environments. Thinkers remain disciplined with their own use of time and are most comfortable under controlled circumstances. They can be skeptical and may even become cynical. They like to see things in writing as a way of measuring or validating expectations and feedback from others.

ON THE OTHER HAND...

Because Thinkers like to be right, they prefer checking processes themselves. This tendency toward perfectionism, when taken to an extreme, can result in "analysis paralysis." These overly cautious traits may result in worry that the process is not progressing exactly right, further promoting their tendency to behave in a critical, detached way.

Thinkers appear to be aloof, meticulous, and critical. Their fear of being wrong can make them over-reliant on the collection of information and slow to reach a decision. While Thinkers are natural observers who ask many questions, they may overly focus on downside possibilities and remote dangers... at the expense of missing up-side opportunities and bottom-line payoffs.

In their effort to avoid conflict, Thinkers often refrain from voluntarily expressing their inner thoughts and feelings. This lack of direct feedback may lead to future misunderstandings and weaken relationship-building opportunities.

DEEP THINKERS

Perhaps you live or work with someone who is quiet, individualistic, painfully slow speaker who covets his or her privacy. Oftentimes, there is a lot going on inside their head as they agonize over what to do next, how their feelings operate, and ultimately, the process of doing what is right. Thinkers tend to put their emotions under a microscope, analyzing and reanalyzing them to make sure they responded appropriately to emotional situations.

THINKERS AT A GLANCE:

Logically and analytical	Need data and to answer questions
Like to be right, correct	Like organization and structure
Prefer objective, task-oriented, intellectual work	Need to understand processes
Make decisions cautiously	Prefer to do things themselves
Work slowly and precisely alone	Like to be admired for their accuracy
Avoid conflict and over-involvement with others	Like to contemplate and reconsider
Like problem solving methods and approaches	Heavily rely on data for decision making

ON THE SOCIAL SCENE WITH THE THINKER

Thinkers contemplate examining the pros and cons of any given situation and trying to consider everything. Their need to weigh possibilities and ramifications can cause stress for other (more impetuous) behavioral types. Sometimes Thinkers consider a situation until the opportunity is missed completely. Yet that innate caution can serve to offset more impetuous ideas or decisions made by the other styles.

Thinkers are astute observers of their surroundings. They virtually absorb everything around them and continually take in and process information. So much so that many Thinkers report having difficulty falling asleep or getting back to sleep if they wake up during the night because they cannot turn off everything that is running through their minds. Thinkers fascinate themselves by processing many of the complexities of life (that often escapes the other types).

Thinkers typically act reserved and distant until they feel they know someone well enough to let down their guard; building trust with them often takes time. They plan and select their relationships cautiously. Because they are such private people, they sometimes seem mysterious or even conniving.

Unlike Socializers, Thinkers do not prefer team sports or group recreational pursuits. On the introverted side, they like to engage in independent indoor and outdoor recreational activities. In the outdoors, you may find them bird watching, kayaking, hiking, camping, or fishing. Indoor activities may include stamp collecting, painting, music, computer games, board games, model building, woodworking, etc. Regardless of the activity, Thinkers often become experts at their hobby or endeavor. Indeed, the one way to get a Thinker to have a conversation is to ask about his or her hobby or recreational pursuit. You may discover that you will learn much more about the subject than you may have ever wanted to know.

Since Thinkers do not readily discuss their feelings or thoughts, their non-verbal responses speak volumes about how they really think or feel. That first little smirk or quick, one-syllable laugh can tell you that they are pleased. Watch the Thinkers' body language for indicators of how they feel about someone or something.

Thinkers are not comfortable telling stories or anecdotes about themselves. When pressed for an opinion or reaction, they may sidestep the issue completely. Asked to "talk about their feelings" is a fearful situation because they are not comfortable doing it.

Thinkers' humor typically shows a down-home, dry, witty perspective, often from an unexpected angle. Perhaps you have seen those comics that deliver the jokes in a deadpan manner; they do not "act funny," but what they say is clever, witty, and point to life's ironies. Bob Newhart and Steven Wright are such comedians; even though they do not express feelings and thoughts easily, they often capture them with timeless stories that contain penetrating insights about human nature.

Small groups of people are much more comfortable for Thinkers since it takes them time to become comfortable with others. They are fearful of mistakes or criticisms and interact with people who pose no threat to them.

Typical social behavior of Thinkers:

- Quiet and observant; likes to collect information before entering a relationship

- Socially cool and distant; waits for other to take the initiative

- Discreet and tactful; not likely to tell secrets or the unadulterated truth

- Serious; suspicious of others unless they have previously proven themselves

- Guarded; prefers a small group of friends and work associates

Preferred social situations of Thinkers:

- Attending a planned, private small gathering of close friends who have consistently proven to be trustworthy in the past

- Participating in organized activities where they can demonstrate and be appreciated for their expertise

- Conversing logically about areas of personal knowledge, adding key input to the conversation

- Talking and listening to ideas and facts rather than feelings

- Conflict-free environments that prize individuality

THINKER'S STYLE AT WORK:

Thinkers prefer careers in which they can strive for perfection, creativity and completeness. The good news is that their attention to detail will help any team plan and execute successful business initiatives. The bad news is that their attention to detail makes it difficult for co-workers to get them see "the big picture."

When you walk into an office that is free from clutter, neatly organized, and notice that the desk is clear except for one file, a phone and maybe a computer, you are likely to be in Thinker territory. Thinkers like neat, sanitized, highly organized desks unimpeded by clutter. Everything in their office has its rightful place as though it was preordained. In fact, if you work with a Thinker (and want to have a little fun), wait until they leave their office and then move one thing on their desk. Soon after returning, the Thinker will notice right away that something is amiss and move the object back to its rightful place. Be advised, never play this prank on the Thinker customer; they will not find it funny.

The office walls of Thinkers contain their favorite types of artwork: charts, graphs, exhibits, models, credentials or more formal, job-related pictures. Thinkers favor a functional decor that enables them to work more efficiently. They tend to keep most resources within reach and readily available whenever needed. However, they tend to keep their materials out of sight and usually locked up to protect their privacy. Where appropriate, you may notice more state-of-the-art technology than with other styles.

Thinkers are non-contact people who prefer the formality of distance. This preference is reflected in the functional arrangement of their desks and chairs, usually with the desks physically separating you from them. They are not natural huggers and touchers, preferring a controlled handshake and brief visits or phone calls. Although they may not keep eye contact with you, do not interpret this to mean they are not interested in what you may be selling. Unemotional, disengaged behavior is common for those who are "Indirect" and "Guarded."

Thinkers often work in these types of positions:

- Forecasters (i.e., political, weather)

- Critics (i.e., film, history, literary)

- Engineers

- Research scientists

- Data analysts

- Accountants/auditors

- Artists/sculptors/architects

- Inventors

- College professors

- Veterinarians

- Technicians and mechanics

Thinkers see themselves as logical problem solvers who like structure, concentrate on key details, and ask specific questions about critical factors. They are masters at following important, established directions and standards, while still meeting the need to control the process by their own actions. Process-oriented Thinkers want to know why something works. Such insight allows them to determine for themselves the most logical way to achieve the expected results from themselves and others.

In business, Thinkers are the refiners of reality. They do not seek utopias nor quick fixes. Because of their risk-averse tendencies, they may overly plan when change becomes inevitable. Planning is their way of improving their odds. They like working in circumstances that promote quality in products or services. When possible, they prepare ahead of time for their projects and then work diligently to perfect them to the highest degree. Their thorough preparation minimizes the probability of errors. They prefer finishing tasks on schedule, but not at the expense of making a mistake. They dislike last minute rushing and inadequate checking or review.

Thinkers prefer logic and rely on reasoning to avoid mistakes. They tend to check, recheck, and check again. They may become mired down with accumulating facts and over-analysis. They are uncomfortable freely giving opinions or partial information until they have exhausted all their resources. This process can frustrate other behavioral types who want to know what is going at the moment.

Whether or not this type opts for a scientific or artistic career, Thinkers often follow a rational method or intuitive, logical progression to achieve their objectives. Because of their natural inclination to validate and improve upon accepted processes, Thinkers tend to generate the most native creativity of the four types. Consequently, they often explore new ways of viewing old questions, concerns and opportunities.

Thinkers seek solace and answers by focusing inwardly. Their natural orientation is toward objects but away from people. From their perspective, people are unpredictable and complicate matters. With more people added to the formula, the chances of getting unpredictable results increase. Thinkers choose to work with colleagues who promote objectivity and thoroughness in the office. When encouraged to do so, Thinkers can share their rich supplies of information with co-workers who can benefit from their wealth of experience and knowledge.

When discussions and tempers become hot and heavy, Thinkers may start looking for an exit… or at least a fallback position to reassess their strategy. They want peace and tranquility, tending to avoid and reject hostility and outward expressions of aggression. They can numb themselves to conflict to such an extent that they may have difficulty tapping into their feelings. They can become perfectionistic and worrisome, both with themselves and with others.

Business characteristics of typical Thinkers:

- Concern with process; want to know how something works

- Intuitive and original; once they know the expected structure, they may invent their own structure, method, or model

- More interested in quality than quantity; prefer lower output to inferior results

- Want to be right; employ logical thinking processes to avoid mistakes

- Sometimes impede progress with their constant checking and rechecking

- Dislike unplanned changes and surprises

- Reject open aggression

Preferred business situations for Thinkers:

- Colleagues and superiors who do not criticize work or ideas, especially in public

- Situations where they can set the quality control standards and check to see if they are properly implemented

- Working with complete information systems or being empowered to formulate their own methods

- Superiors who value correctness and the Thinker's key role in the organization

- Organized and process-oriented workplaces with little emphasis on socializing

THINKER SALESPEOPLE

The natural style of Thinker salespeople is to provide the customer with precise facts and logical information. Because Thinkers are not relationship oriented, they perform best in sales situations involving technical, faster moving products, where buying decisions are based primarily on technical capabilities. Thinkers work well with professional buyers, as they tend to give them an organized, logical presentation, without spending time on small talk.

Thinkers take the time to understand the needs of the customer, as well as the process in which the product or service is expected to perform. Their proposals tend to emphasize the technical features and superiority of their product or service. Thinkers try to provide a "bullet-proof" solution for their customers and are often surprised if the purchase decision is made on other than completely rational basis.

Thinker salespeople are painstaking information gatherers; carefully piece together the needs of the customer and the requirements of the organization before presenting a solution. Their natural style is to depend on their ability to provide solutions rather than focusing on interpersonal relationships. They prefer selling scenarios where they can analyze the situation, map a solution, and then leave any training, installation or follow-up to someone else.

Thinker's E-mails, Letters, and Memos

Thinkers send letters that seek to clarify positions and address processes. Consequently, they may become rather long and filled with information and questions while at the same time they may be somewhat indirect and intentionally obtuse. A second type of Thinker letter is a short communiqué with an accompanying host of enclosures, citations or references. The purpose of their letters is to process information in ways that maintain or enhance their position.

On the Phone with Thinkers

Thinkers are formal, time-conscious, and use the phone as a tool to process tasks whenever necessary. They prefer brief, to-the-point telephone conversations. Thinkers tend to express themselves in a rather tentative manner and display caution in making commitments over the phone. Thinkers speak in a careful, soft manner with non-emotional delivery. While the phone gives them the option to avoid face-to-face involvement, they may perceive unscheduled phone calls as an invasion of their privacy, time, and/or a disruption from their work.

THINKER CUSTOMERS

Thinker customers are task-oriented and need information and specific data to make their decision. Thinkers want to understand the process of the sale, as well as how your hotel will meet the specific criteria they have established with which to make a decision. They need time to evaluate the data. They tend to respond positively to graphs and charts that visually clarify the information. All information presented to Thinkers should be well organized and logical.

Thinkers sometimes become lost in non-essential details that they believe may have some hidden, less obvious significance). Helping them re-focus on the "big picture" and comparative benefits between competing choices can help them towards their decisions.

Thinker customers respond well to efforts to reduce the buying risk. Guarantees, free trials and pilot programs can reduce obstacles to the Thinker's purchasing options. By comparison with the other styles, Thinkers also tend to be concerned about the impact of the purchase decision on the organization; how it fits into policies, procedures, and existing circumstances. Thinkers seldom make their decisions based on only relationships, but it is important that they respect and trust the salesperson and his organization to recover any problems encountered after the purchase.

Thinkers have subdued body language and verbal responses, making them hard to "read." The Thinker is the easiest style to identify because of their low-key, deliberate, measured, and reserved behaviors. They are put off by a perceived excess of either directness or uninformed enthusiasm by salespeople and view too much intensity as distracting and unnecessary. Thinker customers want to know that the salesperson is knowledgeable in his field.

Thinkers prefer a minimum of interaction and prefer a few short phone calls than an intensive series of meetings. Thinker customers tend to avoid personal involvement and are more comfortable with discrete or formal buying procedures.

UPON REFLECTION

Do you know a Thinker? Perhaps it is the person in accounts payable who is slow to respond to questions due to the time it takes for them to process the question and formulate an answer. Is it the night auditor who prefers to work alone at the hotel and wants to spend time working with numbers rather than people? Or is it the housekeeper who shows up to work each day and diligently and quietly follows the checklist for cleaning rooms without need for social interaction with others?

CHAPTER 5

RELATERS:
The Great Helpers

Relaters are warm, supportive and predictable. They are the most group-oriented of all of the four styles. Having friendly, lasting, first name relationships with others is one of their most important desires. They dislike interpersonal conflict to the extent that when they disagree, they will often keep silent. At other times, they may say what they think other people want to hear. They have natural counseling tendencies and are supportive of other people's feelings, ideas, and goals. Others usually feel comfortable interacting with Relaters because of their low-key, non-confrontational nature. As natural listeners, they like to be part of networks of people that share common interests.

RELATERS NEED RESPECT AND TRANQUILITY

Relaters focus on getting acquainted and building trust. They are inwardly frustrated by pushy, aggressive behavior. They are cooperative, steady workers who function well as team members. They strive to maintain stability and to create a peaceful environment. While "venturing into the unknown" may be an intriguing concept for some other types, Relaters prefer to remain with what they already know and have experienced. Risk is a dangerous word to Relaters. They may even stay in an unpleasant environment rather than take chances by making a change. Disruption in their routine patterns can cause them distress. When faced with a change, they need to think it through slowly, systematically, and go step-by-step in preparing for change. Finding elements of sameness within those changes can help minimize their stress.

Relaters yearn for more tranquility and constancy in their lives than the other three types. They operate on an emotional plane that has occasional, moderate mood swings from melancholy to happy. They rarely have emotional highs like that of the Socializer, but the change is noticeable. This reflects their natural need for composure, stability and balance. Their relationships are generally amiable and their relaxed disposition makes them approachable and warm. They are easy-going, calm, and operate at a deliberate, measured pace.

The primary strengths of Relaters are their accommodation, appreciation for – and patience with – others. They are courteous, friendly, and willing to share responsibilities. They are good implementers who are persistent and usually follow-through with the completion of action plan steps; they do so because they hate to let other people down or fear confrontation.

ON THE OTHER HAND...

Relaters have difficulty speaking up and expressing their true feelings, especially if it might create conflict. They appear to go along with others even if they inwardly do not agree. This tendency creates an environment where the more aggressive types may take advantage of the Relater. Their lack of assertiveness sometimes results in hurt feelings because they do not let others know how they truly feel. They can be overly sensitive and easily bullied.

Their need for harmony makes them slower at making decisions as they privately try to find solutions that most likely lead to consensus. People of other styles often view this behavior as weak or indecisive. In fact, their slow but deliberate pace results from their desire to minimize risk in unknown situations, partially by inclusion of others in the decision-making process. Relaters need to stay personally involved in the detailed aspects of work which often causes them to be hesitant to delegate effectively. They often would rather shoulder more work than inconvenience someone else by asking for help.

Relaters are often found in the helping professions: counseling, teaching, social work, ministry, psychology, nursing, and human resources to name a few. Relaters are among the most patient and supportive parents.

THE RELATER AT A GLANCE:

Concern for stability	Think in an orderly manner
Want documentation and facts	Need personal involvement
Take action and make decisions slowly	Need to know the step-by-step sequence
Avoid risks and changes	Dislike interpersonal conflict
Work slowly but cohesively with others	Accommodate others
Want tranquility and peace	Seek security and sense of belonging
Enjoy teamwork	Want to know they are appreciated
Possess excellent counseling talents	Can instantly read if someone is sincere or not

SOCIAL SCENE WITH RELATERS

Relaters are quiet, evenly paced, and inwardly focused individuals. They renew their energy by looking for answers within themselves and a relatively small group of friends, family members and associates. As warm and open as they may appear, they have private thoughts that they are reluctant to divulge. Their energy drains when called upon to share how they feel about private matters or controversial topics that may offend someone. They would rather sit back, observe other's feelings, and then offer a more measured response based on their perception about how their opinion may be received. They are naturally tuned-in to the overall group dynamics as well as the feelings of the individuals that comprise the group.

Relaters are uncomfortable with intangibles. They dislike deviating from the established, proven order, such as when dealing with abstractions. Instead, they prefer to follow a predetermined, straightforward procedure.

They are on firm ground when working with concrete realities, such as known products, people, systems and procedures.

Relaters like routine, predictability, and defined limits. They tend to anchor the other types with their patience, cooperation, and follow-through. They need a firm grip on the facts before feeling ready to proceed; they prefer systematic information whenever possible. They enjoy team efforts and willingly work with others to bolster comfortable, efficient working conditions. Relaters support and encourage other members of their group.

At parties, Relaters like to seek out people they know well and are more likely to attend an event with another invitee with whom they are already comfortable. They often talk with the same person throughout the social function unless they are encouraged to move about more and mingle. They prefer to be approached by others, and often project a serene, accepting attitude that other people often seek them out.

Relaters dislike being in the spotlight and prefer working behind the scenes. They share credit willingly and freely. They choose friends by using the test-of-time method; Relaters tend to have long-lasting relationships. They often keep in touch with childhood friends, former teachers, or even retired doctors. Because familiarity feels so comfortable to them, they may prefer to live in the same neighborhood or area as they did during childhood. Memorabilia tends to mean more to Relaters than for some of the other behavioral styles. Nostalgia makes them feel more connected to the present, giving them a sense of stability even as time passes. Consequently, they tend to be possessive about what they own which has personal significance for themselves and their relationships.

Relaters often use conformity as a means of satisfying their need to feel included by others. They find it easy to listen and have a natural preference for participative communication. One problem facing Relaters is that their aversion to hurting people's feelings may make them respond in an indirect, subtle manner. They find it hard to say "no" and often allow the more assertive types to pressure them. Their willingness to listen makes them shock absorbers or sounding boards for the opinions, ideas, experiences, and frustrations of others.

Relaters tend to continue to work on what they have worked in the past. In most aspects of their lives, what is new or different does not appeal to them as much. The same activities other types perceive as monotonous often appeal to Relaters desire for repetition. For them, familiarity means contentment! They find it difficult to reach beyond their comfort zone and take chances. Although they may remain quiet about resisting change, they may secretly decide to passively revolt.

Relaters display a rather plain, straightforward, seemingly uncomplicated sense of humor. They look at life from a mainstream, commonplace perspective with predictable results. Often, the listener can figure the outcome of their joke before it is completed.

Persistent is a word often used to describe Relaters. They do not give up easily and can persevere for years. This single-minded resolve can be seen as stubbornness!

Relaters are not naturally bothered by little annoyances, overlooking things that bother the other styles. Although Relaters exhibit more patience than many of their counterparts, they sometimes allow certain irritations to build for so long that the burden becomes overwhelming. Because they do not like to be confrontational, they may give in rather than take issue with situations. Relaters bruise easily; you may hurt their feelings without realizing it. Relaters can appear almost saintly, simply because they often keep quiet even when bothered. They do not want anyone to dislike them. They often think that if they say what is on their minds, they may be less likely to keep a friendship. As a result, they will avoid confrontation – their biggest fear—at almost any cost.

Relaters' desire for peace and stability can motivate them to succumb to compromise, maintaining favorable conditions or avoiding conflict. Ironically, instead of jeopardizing their position with others, speaking up and/or taking a stand can sometimes enhance their position... especially with people who may view their tendency to give in as weakness. Voicing their feelings before reaching the end of their tolerance level can actually help Relaters salvage some relationships before it is too late.

Relaters are most comfortable with small groups of people whom they have known for a long time and have had a history of pleasant relationships. They prefer events and activities that are planned or at least known about in advance. This provides them with a more predictable experience with defined dimensions, such as when events start and finish, who will be there, and what activities may occur.

The best social world for Relaters is one where everyone would act friendly, pleasant, and cooperative. A world where nobody would strongly disagree, shout, participate in rowdy scenes, or persuade others to do something against his or her will.

Typical social behaviors for Relaters:

- Building ongoing relationships with a small number of people

- Wanting to be involved in and identified with their group

- Relating to others on one-on-one, preferring predictable role behavior by each person

- More casual, low-keyed, amiable relationships

- Giving and then receiving sincere attention

- Seeking stability in their lives through practices such as conformity

Preferred social situations of Relater:

- Participating in the group's communication and activities

- Performing regular activities in the same way, at the same time, and at the same place such as bowling or golf leagues, bridge club, and poker night.

- Communicating in a conflict-free environment with associates or friends

- Settings that facilitate easy conversations

- Wanting to know how to play games or complete activities

through well-defined, step-by-step procedures

- Feeling appreciated and well-liked by others, just for being who they are

RELATERS STYLE AT WORK

Relaters prefer constancy in their positions and careers. They can focus on learning to specialize in specific areas and be part of a team.

Relater's desks contain pictures of family and friends as well as other personal items. Their office walls display conservatively framed personal slogans, family or group photos, serene pictures, or mementos. They surround themselves with nostalgic memories of stabilizing experiences and relationships. These remembrances of a pleasant, uncomplicated past allow them to transform their offices into a warm, friendly cocoon that shields them from a fast-paced, -changing world.

Relaters prefer to arrange seating in a side-by-side, more congenial, cooperative manner; no big "power desks!" like those preferred by Directors. If they do have a large desk, they will usually walk from behind it to greet their visitors. Colors and furniture selections are generally conventional and conservative in tone. Lighting is usually subdued in their office and decorated with scented candles.

In addition to family photos and pictures, you may find certificates recognizing Relaters for their volunteer hours for various hands-on activities in the community or business. While other behavioral styles may prefer to contribute money, Relaters typically enjoy giving their time for causes they support. Not only does this satisfy their need to give, it provides them an opportunity to meet more potential friends and experience what is going on behind the scenes.

Relaters often work in the following types of positions:

- Financial advisors

- Social workers

- Family doctors/nurses

- Psychologists/counselors

- Residential or community services

- Teachers/professors

- Personal assistants/secretaries

- Insurance agents

- Customer service representatives

In business and in their personal lives, Relaters take one day at a time and may consciously avoid risks and uncertainties. They tend to respect the proven status quo and are likely to accommodate others. Because stability in the workplace motivates them, Relaters are apt to have the most compatible of all working relationships with each of the four types. Relaters have patience, staying power, and persistence; they commit themselves to making relationships work.

Relaters are extremely uncomfortable with conflict and will choose "flight" over "fight" to avoid dealing with it. They do not want to upset the status quo or to appear to be know-it-alls. Silently, they may feel as if they are shouldering most of the duties, but they are unlikely to complain.

When Relaters need to make a presentation, they prepare thoroughly and organize their material in advance. Since they feel comfortable with proven methods, they like to acquaint themselves with each step of a procedure so they can duplicate it later. Sometimes, when this is taken to extreme, this adherence to following instructions and maintaining the status quo can limit their effectiveness.

Relater's patience and inclination to follow procedures makes them a natural choice for assisting or tutoring others, maintaining existing performance levels, and organizing practices. They often enjoy setting up or implementing guidelines or checklists that enable others to be more organized in their follow-through efforts.

Relaters prefer to resolve problems by working with others as part of a team and using time tested methods. If these tactics fail, Relaters may quietly do nothing. When conflict and stress increase, Relater's tolerance may decrease, resulting in lowered performance or even absenteeism as a way of coping with the stress.

Relationships, which provide them with security, friendliness, and large doses of routine, attract Relaters. Teaching is a natural career for them since it satisfies their natural desire for helping people.

Inherently modest and accommodating, Relaters usually think their actions speak for themselves. Inwardly, they may want to divulge a personal triumph, but they will not volunteer it or brag about it. Rather than asking for a promotion, Relaters will quietly hope the supervisor notices their good work and offers them a reward.

Since Relaters seek security and inclusion within a group, they can contribute to the workplace with their natural organizing talents, consistent pace, and desire to fit in. They favor work relationships on a casual, first name basis, and enjoy developing more in-depth friendships with selected co-workers. They contribute to harmony in the office, but they sometimes become overly dependent on using the same methods repeatedly even when they work less and less effectively.

Relaters are the optimistic realists among the four styles. As pragmatists in this regard, they like to do what is routine with familiar people to maintain the same situation. They perform regularly and deliberately toward this end of holding on to continuity, peace, and orderliness. Changes and surprises make them uncomfortable because they alter the current formulas. Relaters prefer refinement over dramatic changes.

Typical business characteristics of Relaters:

- Need to know the order of procedures; fears the unknown

- Build strong, deep, slow and steady relationships with fewer people

- Operate well as a member of the work group

- Motivated by customary, known, proven practices

- An orientation toward more concrete, repeatable actions

- Want order and stability in the workplace

- A focus on how and when to do things

- Work in a steady and predictable manner

- Like a long-term relationship with their place of business and their fellow employees

Preferred business situations of Relaters:

- Performing the same kinds of duties day after day despite the importance of the type of work involved

- Working cooperatively with others to achieve common results

- Enjoying safe, risk-free environments with a minimum of changes

- Knowing each step toward completing their duties within a defined framework of time and resources

- Making decisions by group consensus or other accepted practices rather than only by themselves

- Feeling like an appreciated, contributing member of the work group

RELATER SALESPEOPLE

The natural style of Relater salespeople is to build relationships and to progress slowly and steadily through the sales process. They are very concerned with maintaining the relationship and making sure that they have the best possible solution for their customer. They spend a great deal of time getting to know the customer personally and seeking to understand their personal preferences and dislikes. They also use their listening talents to understand the needs and wants of the customers.

The Relaters ideal sales position requires strong customer relationships and a service orientation. Systems or services that require months (or years) of repeated, incremental work to respond to known needs (and involve the same decision makers) are perfect for Relaters. They maintain relationships with high levels of service, personal involvement, and attention to details.

Relater salespeople seldom push for a close. But their painstaking emphasis on knowing and understanding the needs and expectations of customers leads naturally to the customer's commitment to do business with the hotel.

Relaters are most successful working in sales and catering to give them the time required to plan an event that meets the needs and expectations of the customer. They tend to provide their customers with plenty of input to finalize the purchase decision. They enjoy sales or service work that requires a team approach.

One weakness of Relater salespeople needs to be noted. While it is true that their greatest strength is reading others, it can get in the way when working toward confirming a sale. They become worried about applying too much pressure or what may happen to the customer after the sale. They ask themselves, "What happens if the bride is unhappy with the table settings selected for the wedding reception? I would feel just terrible if they were not completely happy." This issue is one that a Relater salesperson must learn to deal with to become more successful.

Relaters E-mails, Letters and Memos

Relaters send letters to update people or keep in touch. Relaters like to send thank you notes for almost anything: inviting them to an office party, bringing lunch back for them, or including them on a company function. They may even send a thank you note to acknowledge your thank you note. You can count on holiday season cards from them every year as you remain in a relationship with them.

On the Phone with Relaters

Relaters greet people warmly on the phone, asking, "How are you?" and expressing pleasure at hearing from you. They immediately put you on a first-name basis and patiently listen to your ideas and feelings. Relaters talk more slowly and quietly with a steady, even-tempered delivery. They enjoy listening; it affords them another avenue to best understand and respond to others. Yet make no mistake: face-to-face interaction is always preferable to the phone.

RELATER CUSTOMERS

Relater customers need to have a relationship based upon personal assurances and trust prior to making a buying decision. Such Relaters tend to assemble a buying committee of advisors to help them make the decision because they want everyone affected by the purchase to stay involved in the decision. Relaters are seldom in a hurry to make decisions and will become turned off by pushy, aggressive behavior.

Relater customers respond to friendly attention and efforts to make them feel like a member of the family by the sales team. They need to be personally at ease with the salesperson. They also want to understand how the operations of the company behind the salesperson might affect them. They want the salesperson to listen and be sensitive to their needs and situational requirements. Once they have established a strong relationship, they are likely to remain loyal to the salesperson despite potential competition.

Relater customers expect salespeople to be available to make presentations to other people within the organization who might have an interest in the purchasing decision. They want to make sure that the decision will be completely accepted by their organization before making a final commitment. They also want assurance that they can depend on the salesperson to honor all commitments.

They have difficulty saying "no" and may make excuses or create delays to get out of a difficult sales situation. Relaters expect the salesperson to be in tune with their needs and feelings. When they perceive that the salesperson is not being sincere, they may withdraw or change the subject. There is one exception to this tendency: Relaters will say "no" rather quickly when they get the sense that a hotel salesperson is lying or trying to suggest they do something that may be harmful to their company, family or personal security.

UPON REFLECTION

Perhaps you know a Relater in the sales office. Is it the person who is genuinely interested in how everyone is doing in the office each day? Is it the salesperson that has genuine relationships with customers and rewarded with steady business? Is he or she the one who is always making sure everybody feels welcome by the sales team? Is she the one who knows instantly when a prospective customer is disingenuous and trying to cheat the hotel? Is she highly regarded for her community service work to help those in need? If so, this member of the sales team is probably a Relater.

SECTION II

IDENTIFYING
THE FOUR BEHAVIORAL STYLES

In this section, you will learn two simple techniques that will get you well on your way to determining the behavioral styles of others. You will discover ways to determine whether each individual is more Direct or Indirect and more Open or Guarded. In doing so, you can quickly determine whether each customer is a Director, Socializer, Thinker, or Relater.

CHAPTER 6

IDENTIFYING YOUR CUSTOMER'S STYLE

Our sales technique is based upon observable behaviors, NOT "personalities" or "temperaments." Such a distinction is critical because people may often change their behavior in the middle of a conversation. When you learn to adapt to the behavior that you are witnessing, you will maintain rapport with that person. People's personalities are deeply ingrained and slow to change, but behaviors can change quickly. The way a person is acting at each moment in time will dictate how you should be selling to them.

There are two "dimensions" that help us determine another person's style:

1. How "Direct" or "Indirect" the behaviors are, and;

2. How "Open" or "Guarded" one is in revealing private thoughts.

When you correctly read both of these dimensions, you have determined the other person's natural style and are heading in the right direction for an effective relationship.

DIRECT BEHAVIORS

The dimension of "directness" deals with the amount of involvement a person uses to meet his needs by seeking to influence people and situations. Directness means the tendency to move forward, outwardly expressing thoughts, feelings or expectations.

Direct people, to borrow a Wall Street metaphor, are the "bulls." They can be forcefully expressive, Type-A personalities who confront conflict, change, risk, and decision-making head on without giving it a second thought.

Direct people are outspoken communicators and often dominate business meetings. They will tell you their opinions even if you do not want to hear them; if they want your opinion, they will give it to you!

Direct people are competitive, impatient, and sometimes confrontational. They bulldoze or zoom their way through life. They often argue for the sake of arguing. They hold eye contact longer than average and possess an air of confidence. Their handshakes are memorable for their firmness.

Direct people thrive on accomplishment and are not overly concerned with rules and policies. They are more likely to look for expedient ways to attain their goals rather than to focus on obstacles or setbacks. Ambiguity does not deter them but encourages them. They take advantage of gray areas and call them "windows of opportunity."

Direct people come on strong, taking social initiative and creating powerful first impression. They tend to be assertive, fast-paced people who make swift decisions and take risks. They can easily become impatient with others who do not keep up with their pace. As active people who talk a lot, they appear confident and sometimes dominant. Direct people tend to express opinions readily and make emphatic statements. Such individuals try to shape their environment and relationships directly. "Tell Stevenson that I want to talk to him ASAP!" barks a Direct person; a more Indirect person may ask his secretary to see if Mr. Stevenson would please come to his office when it is convenient.

Direct people are faster paced, more assertive, and more competitive than Indirect people. At worst, these tendencies sometimes transform into hastiness, combativeness, or a lower awareness of others' needs. More outspoken, talkative, and dominant, Direct people are extroverts who focus their attention on interests within their immediate environment. They tend to work and play faster. When at a social gathering, they are the ones who introduce themselves as a natural way of seeking to influence others.

Direct people prefer to make rapid decisions, often becoming impatient when the process does not move fast enough or does not go their way. Checking for errors is something other people can do; it's too time-consuming and self-involving for Direct people. Instead of checking, they busily rush into new areas where those who are more Indirect may fear to tread. In fact, they often rush into so many new areas that their time seems to evaporate into thin air. They often run late to meetings and appointments because they are easily distracted. Meanwhile, their more punctual, Indirect colleagues have learned to expect Direct people to be late so prepared to pass the time waiting for their sidetracked colleagues by playing with their smartphones, flipping through magazines, and so forth.

Direct people may enjoy taking risks and want immediate results now. Risks are a way of life for them; they find enjoyment in going against the status quo. They crave excitement, so they do as much as possible to get it.

Direct people grow impatient with a slow decision-making process. They prefer to make a quick decision to address a problem and then implement it to see what happens. "Who cares if the output isn't perfect, did it work?" they ask. If so, the desired result was achieved. The quantity of decisions made (based on a quota known only to them) beats quality most days of the week. Therefore, they are likely to tolerate a higher error rate than their Indirect counterparts because they figure that the number of successes is more important than the percentage of successes. They play for high stakes results.

Direct people are the "home run" crushers, not "get on base," high-average hitters. Direct people "swing for the fences" with gusto! They focus on the one-in-ten grand slam while quickly erasing the memories of the strikeouts that occur between connecting with the "big one." If the hotel is having a sales contest, you can be sure this person will obsess over winning it!

Anyone involved in hotel sales realizes that the road to success is littered with rejection and setbacks, especially when spending the morning doing "smile and dial" to talk to current or prospective customers. Direct people excel at these jobs because they are able to handle rejection as they work diligently to get to the customer who says "Yes, I am looking to book an event." They know that the odds of getting to a "Yes" increase as they work through the "No's." Indirect people tend to take "No" as personal rejection responding by preferring other tasks that do not force them into risk-taking. Indirect salespeople say, "Maybe if I send out an e-mail, then follow up by phone, I'll increase my chances of getting a positive response." Indirect salespeople sometimes invest too much time and effort in low-payoff marketing activities (i.e., sending letters and brochures) because it is "selling indirectly" without having to handle rejection from customers.

Direct people point, finger jab, or otherwise more observably express themselves. They are verbally intense and expressive. "Take it or leave it," Direct people exclaim. "This is the way it is going to be so get used to it!" They emphasize their points of view with confident-sounding vocal intonations and assertive body language.

Speaking with conviction, fast-talking, Direct people like to tell – not ask – about situations. If you want to know the answer, simply ask them. They can even become brutally blunt: "Are you sure that is a custom suit? It looks more like a horse blanket ... ha, ha, ha. I'm just kidding, of course!" While other Direct types might join in the laughter, Indirect people are sensitive to feelings and likely to be thinking, "Gosh, I wonder what would possess someone to come right out and say something hurtful like that?"

Impatient and quick-paced, Direct people jump into things, so they get into more "iffy" situations than their Indirect counterparts. Sometimes they net huge results and sometimes they encounter dramatic disasters. They have difficulty following established policies and procedures believing that there is nothing wrong with doing things their way as long as they reach their sales goals. The truly Direct person's motto might be, "It is easier to ask forgiveness than seek permission."

When windows of opportunity open, Direct types cannot wait to tell somebody about their idea or plan of action. Therefore, they seek willing listeners – usually of the Indirect variety – about the opportunity... even if it includes a gray area in policies and procedures. Indirect types listen and often reply with a cautious, "It sounds interesting, but it also raises a lot of questions. Have you asked anyone else for their opinion… like the boss?"

Summary: Remember… one "dimension" is not "better" than the other. People who are more Direct in their behavior have certain advantages than those who are Indirect. However, they also have disadvantages, especially when dealing with people who are less Direct than themselves.

Indirect Behaviors

On the opposite end of the Directness spectrum, one finds the quieter and reserved group… the Indirect people. They may seem to be more easygoing or at least more self-contained in keeping their views to themselves. Indirect people ask questions and listen more than they talk. They typically do not share their opinions or concerns. When asked to take a stand, they may either make tentative statements or say nothing at all. They often appear more objective, introverted, and indecisive.

Indirect people are Wall Street "bears." They approach risk, decision-making, and change cautiously. They are the "meek who inherit the earth." They are the Type-B personalities who are slow-paced and low-key in their approach with others.

Indirect people are tentative, reserved communicators. They are not eager, high-profile contributors in meetings although their insights can be very valuable. When solicited for their opinions, they often preface their statements with qualifications such as: "Have we all considered what might happen if…" or "According to the theories/principles of…"

Indirect people avoid open conflict whenever possible. They are more diplomatic, patient, and cooperative. On unimportant issues, they will conform rather than argue. When they have strong convictions about an issue, however, they will stand their ground… often simply by withholding the approval sought from them. They often base their delays on the need for additional research, pending contracts, or missing data. When they are less than completely convinced, they subconsciously weigh an issue's importance against the discomfort of confrontation.

Indirect people are low profile, reserved, and gentle. For example, their handshakes are sometimes soft; they speak at a slower pace and lower volume than direct people. They do not take the initiative at social gatherings but prefer to wait for others to approach them.

When taken to an extreme, these positive traits can be viewed as negative ones: indecisive, tight-lipped, unassertive behaviors. Indirect people act in a less confronting, less demanding, less assertive, and less socially competitive manner than their Direct counterparts. They allow others to take the social initiative. For instance, when they want to go to the movies or a restaurant, they might think to themselves, "I'd rather see that new romantic-comedy movie." However, when their spouse or date suggests the latest action-adventure epic, they often go along without mentioning their own interests. If they truly disagreed with the suggestion, they may go so far as to say, "Gee, I heard that other movie was really well received. Are you sure you wouldn't rather try that one tonight?" Usually, their desires remain unspoken.

Indirect people tend to be more sensitive toward risk: moving cautiously, meditating on their decisions, and avoid major changes. As a result, they often avoid taking bold chances or acting spontaneously. After all, what is the best way to keep from failing? One way is to do nothing until you are convinced it will be an improvement. Sure things result in a higher success ratio, so they are choices that are more attractive for Indirect people.

When Indirect people fail, they tend to take the setback personally. They are likely to internalize or privately reassess any failure, often wondering if there's something wrong with them. "How could I have been so stupid?" the Indirect asks himself after a setback. Give them a hint that something is going wrong, and reserved people may engage in negative self-talk for days. In contrast, Direct types seldom spend looking back and reflecting on such considerations.

Indirect people tend to move at a slower, more measured pace than Direct people. They speak and respond more slowly since they are more cautious or stability-focused when considering change. They tend to seek increases in security while looking for ways to reduce fear. If their behavior becomes too measured, detractors (usually Direct people) may view this as procrastination or a lack of interest.

Predictability is more important to such Indirect people; they tend to weigh pros and cons, attend to details, and fact-find. Caught in a gray area with no clear-cut guidelines, they usually ask for clarification or permission before they take action. They seek to meet their needs by accommodating the requirements of their environment. They tend to operate according to established formats and rules. When you make an appointment with Indirect people, you can expect them to show up on time, if not early!

Indirect people tend to communicate by asking or observing instead of stating or showing. Their questions attempt to clarify, support, or seek more information. They prefer qualified statements and speak more tentatively, often taking a roundabout or systematic approach. "According to some sources," or "It seems to like/as though," and "Perhaps another way of looking at this situation might be to consider...," are common ways Indirects preface a comment, idea, or opinion. If they do not like something, they respond subtly: "Well, other people have often commented about how good you look in your navy pinstripe suit." This is an Indirect's way of telling you she dislikes the brown suit you are wearing. They reserve the right to express their opinions or keep them to themselves.

READING BEHAVIORAL STYLES

In this next section, we will describe a quick way to identify your style and the styles of others. In doing so, you are on your way to having better relationships with people at work, home, and in social settings.

As you seek to know your style and that of others, bear in mind that people are complex creatures. Every person possesses each of the styles to some degree. However, people do have one dominant style that surfaces above the other three that gives them their uniqueness. There are instances where a person may be Direct in one setting (such as work) but Indirect when at home; they may be Open with their significant other, yet Guarded with co-workers. Be prepared to deal with the person in the behavior that they are demonstrating at the particular moment when interacting with them.

Before you learn how to "read" the behavioral styles of others, identify your own style. In the chart below, you will find a chart listing Indirect and Direct behaviors. Read each pair of descriptive behaviors and check the one that most closely describes your behavior. For example, do you tend to "avoid risks" or "take risks?" Check the one that most describes your behavior. Remember, **one is not "better" than the other**; this is simply a way to begin developing the skill of reading your behavioral style and that of others.

Check here if this behavior sounds most like you	Indirect Behaviors	or	Direct Behaviors	Check here if this behavior sounds most like you
	I tend to be slower paced.	or	I tend to be faster paced.	
	I tend to listen more than talk.	or	I tend to talk more than listen.	
	I am reluctant to directly express my opinions.	or	I find it easy to directly express my opinions.	
	I usually react slowly when faced with new situations or decisions.	or	I usually react quickly when faced with new situations or decisions.	
	I make decisions after all the facts are available.	or	I make decisions whether or not all the facts are available.	
	I come across as less assertive than others.	or	I come across as more assertive than others.	
	I tend to "bite my tongue" when I don't agree with someone.	or	I tend to "speak my mind" when I don't agree with someone.	
	I get frustrated when things move too quickly.	or	I get impatient when things move too slowly.	
	I generally avoid conflict.	or	I do not avoid conflict.	
	Total Indirect Behaviors		**Total Direct Behaviors**	

Now that you have completed the list, are you more Indirect or more Direct? Keep this in mind to determine your behavioral style after you read the next section on whether you behave in a more "Open" or "Guarded" manner that will enable you to identify your behavioral style and that of other people. Especially when those people are prospective customers!

OPEN OR GUARDED?

Do They Wear Their Heart On Their Sleeve… or Hide a Card Up Their Sleeve?

While Direct individuals attempt to control the people around them, Indirect types prefer to exercise control of their environment. In addition to Direct/Indirect, the other dimension of observable behavior that people tend to exhibit is Open or Guarded. This second behavioral scale explains the internal motivating goals behind our daily actions. The Open/Guarded dimension relates to why we what we do in the way we do unto them. When combined, these two scales explain both the tendency to reveal our thoughts and feelings in addition to the degree to which we tend to support other people's expressions of their thoughts and feelings.

OPEN BEHAVIORS

Open people are motivated by their relationships and feelings. They get to know people and tend to make decisions based on feelings, experiences, and relationships.

Open people often become physically and emotionally closer to others. During a conversation, they may almost stand on your toes. They are huggers, hand shakers, "touchers," and smile naturally. They are outgoing and develop deeper relationships with others.

Open people are informal. They like to exchange first names as soon as possible, preferring relaxed, warm relationships. Open people enjoy free-flowing, enjoyable conversations. They can often be as interested in your brother-in-law's surgery as they are in discussing the business on the formal agenda. Interaction within a conversation is more important than content to time constraints.

Additionally, Open people dislike time constraints and rarely mind when other people consume much of their time. In fact, they often balk at imposed schedules and agendas.

Open people are feeling-oriented decision makers. They are in touch with their intuitions as well as the feelings of others. They come to their decisions through their interaction with others rather than their own thoughts.

Open people are emotionally available and show it by talking with their body, using more vocal inflections, making continual eye contact, and communicating in terms of feelings more than the Guarded types. Other Open clues are animated facial expressions, lots of hand and body movement, a flexible time perspective, and immediate non-verbal feedback. Open people also like to tell or listen to stories and anecdotes, making personal contact. They are comfortable with emotions and openly express their joy, sadness, confusion, and other feelings.

Open people respond to passing interests—their own and that of others'—even though this may take them away from the business or subject at hand. They like to make conversations enjoyable so they will share personal experiences and interests seemingly unrelated to the topic being discussed. For example, during a business meeting an Open person might say, "That reminds me of the time my uncle Jed got stuck on the Garden State Freeway in a snowstorm!" leaving others wondering how it relates to the topic of conversation.

Open types are also more accepting about time usage. Their time perspective is organized around the needs of people first and tasks second, so they are more flexible about how others use their time than the Guarded types. "I'm sorry I'm late," explains an Open person, "but Jimmy was crying this morning because Jason broke his science project. I had to write a note to his teacher and cheer him up before I dropped him off at school."

Guarded Behaviors

Guarded people are harder to read than Open people. Guarded types like to conceal their emotions in order to increase their probability of getting the upper hand and decreasing the probability of appearing foolish. Guarded types are motivated by completing tasks and accomplishing their goals.

Guarded people are slow to share their emotions and appear to be more physically rigid and less expressive than Open people. They like to present an image of being in control and not frustrated by other people or situations. If you were a stand-up comedian, you would not want an audience full of Guarded people. Like most of their emotions, their laughter is kept primarily on the inside.

Guarded people keep their distance physically, emotionally, and psychologically. They are harder to get to know than Open types. They tend to remain aloof and value their privacy, especially at the beginning of a relationship. They arrange their offices to provide formal efficiency and a comfortable distance from visitors. They prefer to keep on a professional, business level, when interacting with strangers.

Guarded people are task-oriented. A conversation with a Guarded person will rarely stray from the topic that initiated the contact. They dislike interruptions from their agendas unless they initiate the diversion.

Guarded people are fact-oriented decision makers. They respond to proof and hard evidence. In the workplace, they prefer to work alone and put less emphasis on opinions and feelings of others. On the surface, they appear to operate in an intellectual rather than an emotional mode.

Guarded people are champions of time management. They are efficiency experts who create and follow rigid plans and schedules. They implore other people to respect their time and not to waste it.

Guarded people tend to stand further away from you (even when shaking hands) than Open types. They have a strong sense of personal space and dislike when someone invades their territory. They feel violated when something is taken from their desk, use personal items without permission, or call meetings that require their time without asking their input.

Guarded people show less facial expression, display limited or controlled hand and body movements, and adhere to a more time-disciplined agenda. They push for facts and details, focusing on the issues and tasks. They keep their personal feelings private. They are not naturally "touchy-feely," and they tend to respond stiffly if anyone touches them. They give less wide-ranging, non-verbal feedback unlike their Open counterparts.

In contrast to Open people, Guarded people prefer working on tasks rather than working with people. Typical comments from Guarded people include, "I can't talk now, Frank," or "I have a two o'clock deadline to meet," or "I'll let you know when I have time to do that." or "I'll get back to you later after I've had more time to think about it."

Guarded people like structure and know what is expected of them. Additionally, they prefer to have control over results within a structured environment. They can be viewed as coercive, restrictive, or overbearing when motivated negatively. They prefer to follow the agenda, especially when it is their own!

Because time equals money to Guarded individuals, they are more disciplined about how other people use their time. In part, this explains their tendency not to show, discuss, or willingly listen to thoughts and feelings to the extent of Open people. Guarded types are more matter-of-fact, with more fixed expectations of people and situations. Just as facts place second for Open people, feelings are less important for Guarded people. You might say that Open people tend to experience life by tuning in to the concerns or feeling states of themselves and others and then reacting to them. By contrast, Guarded people focus on the tasks or ideas in question and respond primarily to those stimuli.

Guarded people prefer to know where a conversation is heading. Idle, non-directed small talk is uncomfortable for them. If Open types stray from the subject, Guarded people find a way to bring them back on track. They usually need clarity before they move on to the next topic. If you get off the subject, they are likely to ask, "Can you sum that up for me?" or "What is the key point you're trying to make?"

Because of their different priorities, Guarded people often perceive Open people as inefficient or indecisive. Conversely, Open people may view Guarded people as cold, unsympathetic, or self-involved. As a result, misunderstandings can quickly develop when we do not discern and respond to the source of the differences – the inner motivating needs that drive our personal styles of behavior.

TYPICAL BEHAVIORS

In the next chart, you will find a checklist for Open and Guarded behaviors. Read each pair of behavior descriptions on the list and check the ones that most closely describe you. For example, are you more "relaxed, warm and animated" or more "formal and proper?" Check the one that describes you. Then do the same for each pair of descriptors. As with the previous checklist, remember that one is not "better" than the other; it is simply a way of beginning to develop the skill of reading the behavioral style of others.

Check here if this behavior sounds most like you	Open Behaviors	or	Guarded Behaviors	Check here if this behavior sounds most like you
	I find it easy to share and discuss personal feelings with others.	or	I prefer to keep personal feelings private, sharing them only when necessary.	
	I prefer to socialize with others before getting tasks started.	or	I prefer getting tasks completed before socializing with others.	
	I tend to exhibit animated facial expressions during conversations with others.	or	I tend NOT to exhibit animated facial expressions during conversations with others.	
	I tend to get motivated when dealing with people on a daily basis.	or	I tend to get stressed when dealing with people on a daily basis.	
	I prefer to work with other people or in groups.	or	I prefer to work independently.	
	I am easy to approach in new social situations.	or	I am more standoffish in new social situations.	
	I am easy to get to know.	or	It takes time to get to know me.	
	I value feelings over facts.	or	I value facts over feelings.	
	I usually am NOT time disciplined.	or	I am mostly time disciplined.	
Total Open Behaviors			**Total Guarded Behaviors**	

Now that you have completed both checklists, you can determine your behavioral style:

- If you rated yourself as "Open" and "Direct," you are a Socializer.
- If you rated yourself as "Guarded" and "Direct," you are a Director.
- If you rated yourself as "Indirect" and "Open," you are a Relater.
- If you rated yourself as "Indirect" and "Guarded," you are a Thinker.

Another way to verify your self-assessment is by taking the online assessment at www.alessandra.com/taassessments.asp. If the results match, you may be well on your way to identifying your behavioral style and the first step to becoming a more successful salesperson.

EXAMPLES FOR READING CUSTOMERS STYLES

The best way to learn how to read the behavioral style of customers is to demonstrate the process using a hotel sales example. Remember that each new encounter, whether in person or over the phone, should begin with you seeking answers to the two basic questions that will help you get a sense of the other person's behavioral style. **Is the customer "Open or Guarded?" Is the customer "Direct or Indirect?"** The answers to these two questions will enable you to adapt to the style of that individual from that point forward to increase rapport, improving your probability of booking an event at your hotel.

Imagine you are a salesperson preparing for a sales meeting with a third-party meeting planner who needs to book a corporate event at your hotel. When you originally called Ms. Jones, her voice sounded impatient and rushed; she talked rapidly. She quickly told you that she was very busy but needed to meet with you as soon as possible to sort out the details a two-day business conference for a prestigious client who accepted her RFP. Your hotel was referred to her from a trusted colleague and nobody was going to get the business but you, but you had better be prepared to offer a competitive bid and answer all her questions to her satisfaction without hesitation.

On the drive over to meet Ms. Jones, you can reflect on the phone conversation and note she has already exhibited several "Direct" traits: she talked fast, did most of the talking, and wanting a competitive bid for her business. Her continuum checklist may look similar to the one below:

Check here if this behavior sounds most like you	Indirect Behaviors	or	Direct Behaviors	Check here if this behavior sounds most like you
	She appeared to be slower paced.	or	She appeared to be faster paced.	**X**
	She listened more than talk.	or	She talked more than listen.	**X**
	She often made qualified statements: "According to my sources…" or, "I think in some cases…"	or	She often made emphatic statements: "This is so!" or, "I'm quite positive that…"	
	She appeared to be patient and/or cooperative.	or	She appeared to be impatient and/or competitive.	**X**
	She offered a weak handshake and looked away often during your conversation.	or	She offered a strong handshake and confidently maintained eye contact throughout the conversation.	
	Her questions tended to be for clarification, support and/or to gain more information.	or	Her questions seemed to be rhetorical… to emphasize points or to challenge information.	
	She used very subdued hand gestures and spoke in a rather quiet, monotone voice.	or	She frequently used hand gestures and voice intonations while making points.	
0	**Total Indirect Behaviors**		**Total Direct Behaviors**	**3**

You now refer to the Platinum Grid below and start to think where she might fit. To really make the best decision, you will need to make more observations.

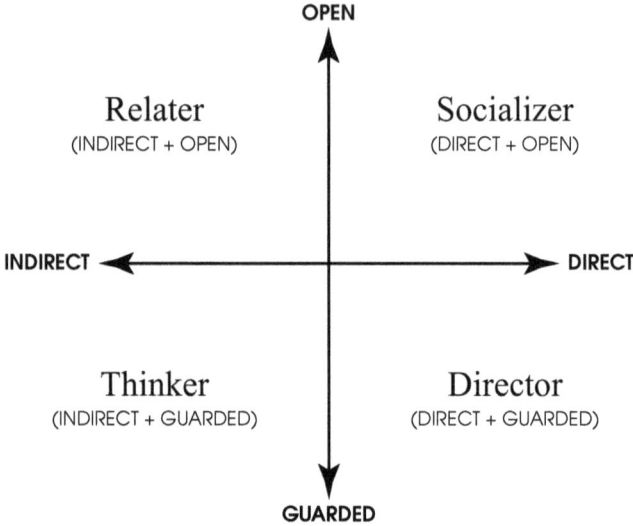

Although a few items on the checklist could not be determined prior to your first meeting, your best indication at this point is that she is a Direct person. You will make a better determination once you have the opportunity to meet her in person. Once you have made the decision that Ms. Jones is Direct, you have effectively eliminated the two styles that fall on the left side of the Platinum Grid.

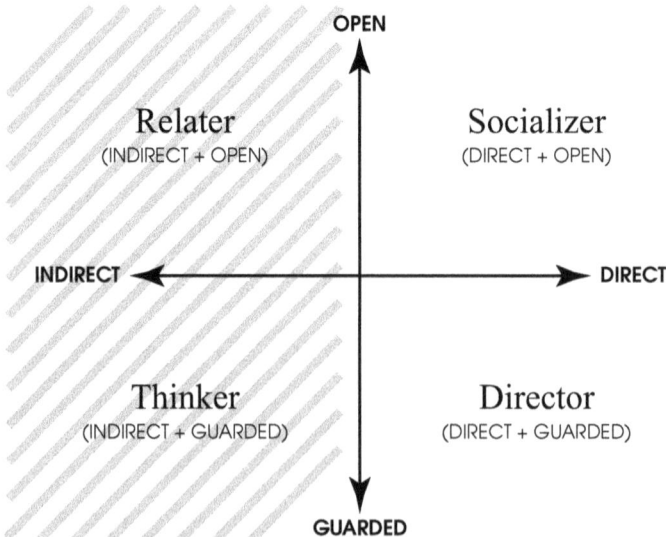

Since you think Ms. Jones is Direct, she must either be a Socializer or a Director. Your best guess is soon confirmed; as you enter the door, you are offered a seat at Ms. Jones's heavy oak worktable and she gets right down to business. There are no pleasantries or small talk; she gets right down to business! You look around the room and notice it to be quite masculine with a large wooden desk, leather chair, diplomas on the wall, and a trophy for winning a recent 5k. She is very task-oriented as you go over the specifications of the RFP. Now that the meeting is under way, you can now refer to the Open versus Guarded continuum checklist.

Check here if this behavior sounds most like you	Open Behaviors	or	Guarded Behaviors	Check here if this behavior sounds most like you
	It seemed easy for her to share and discuss her personal feelings with you.	or	She preferred to keep her personal feelings private, sharing them only when necessary.	X
	She seemed comfortable socializing with you before getting down to business.	or	She got right down to business and made little effort to socialize.	X
	She exhibited animated facial expressions during the conversation.	or	She exhibited very little facial expression during the conversation.	X
	Her conversation often strayed from the subject at hand.	or	She focused the conversation on the relevant issues and stayed on subject.	X
	She came across as warm and relaxed.	or	She came across as cool, formal and proper	
	She walked out to greet you, offering a warm handshake at a close distance.	or	Her greeting was "officious" (a quick handshake offered from a distance).	
	She didn't seem to notice the passing of time.	or	She seemed to keep a sharp eye on the time.	X
0	**Total Open Behaviors**		**Total Guarded Behaviors**	**5**

Based on referencing both checklists, it is readily apparent that Ms. Jones is Guarded and Direct, which leads you to conclude that she is more likely to be a Director. If you have not done so already, you need to stay strictly to the business at hand and have prompt answers to all her questions. Otherwise, she may begin to question the reason you were referred to her in the first place meaning you risk losing the business if her confidence is shaken.

Here is another example. You call Sam Greenwood, the vice president of a large financial institution (which should already start to narrow down his behavioral style based on his occupation), to set up an appointment to discuss a full day business meeting at your hotel that will include meeting rooms and meal functions. Mr. Greenwood answers his own phone in a notably quiet voice. He talks in a soft, moderately paced tone and listens patiently as you explain who recommended that you call. After your introduction, he spends a minute or two talking about his friendship with the person who referred you. He asks several questions about your company and you. He addresses you by your first name. When you ask for an appointment, he says his schedule is flexible and asks what time would be convenient for you.

Again, using the process of elimination, you look at the descriptors of Direct versus Indirect and decide that Mr. Greenwood's soft voice, patience, and the amount of time he spent listening places him on the Indirect side of the dimension. That eliminates the behavioral styles on the right side of the quadrant: Socializer and Director. When you look at the Open versus Guarded descriptions, you remember that Mr. Greenwood spent time talking about his friendship with the person who referred you, he seemed interested in getting to know more about you, he had a warm, friendly tone, and he was flexible about setting up a meeting time convenient for you. You decide that he must be more Open than Guarded. By combining Indirect and Guarded, you determine that Mr. Greenwood is a Relater (and perhaps a Thinking-Relater given his occupation).

Let us look at another scenario. You and your team are doing a sales blitz for the holiday season. You have put together a small goodie bag with hot cocoa, snowflakes, a biscotti, candy canes, promotional packages, and contact information. Your team calls on a car dealership to speak to the sales manager about your promotion. You are introduced to the sales manager and he happily invites you into his office, which is decorated with all sorts of pictures, mismatched furniture, and stacks of papers everywhere. Before you can even ask the manager if he is planning a staff Christmas party, he begins to speak rapidly with lots of hand gestures, saying how happy he is you visited and what a beautiful day it is outside.

He then goes off on a tangent about his recent trip to Vegas and encourages your sales team to go to Vegas, too.

There is no doubt he is behaving in a Direct manner because he is doing all the talking, listening halfheartedly, and using hand gestures. Due to the process of elimination, you know you are dealing with a Director or Socializer. The final determination is how little the individual time spends talking about the business at hand as he talks about himself in a loose, unstructured, fun way indicating Open behavior. Given those additional behavioral cues, you would be correct in determining this Direct and Open person to be a Socializer, keeping in mind the environmental cues of the office, which are definitely different than that of most Directors.

Now determine who it is in your personal or professional life that fit the profile of each of the four styles. If you can come up with examples of those who epitomize each of the styles you will find it increasingly easier to read those you already know or meet for the first time. Once you get into the habit, you will find it almost impossible NOT to read the behavioral styles of your customers. Like so many who have learned to read behavioral styles, you will wonder why you did not pick up on it earlier in your sales career and how that may have impacted the overall sales performance of your hotel to date.

TEST YOUR ABILITY TO IDENTIFY BEHAVIORAL STYLES

Before we move on to the next section of the book, quiz yourself to see if you can identify Open versus Guarded behaviors and Indirect versus Direct behaviors. In doing so, you will find reading behavioral styles easier. Try not to look at the answers below until you have answered the following questions. For each item, mark an X under the Direct or Indirect heading.

Direct or Indirect?

	Indirect		Direct
1. Talks Fast	_____	or	_____
2. Listens Carefully	_____	or	_____
3. Firm Handshake	_____	or	_____
4. Speaks Softly	_____	or	_____
5. Uses Emphatic Gestures	_____	or	_____
6. Asks Clarification Questions	_____	or	_____
7. Longer Eye Contact	_____	or	_____
8. Makes Tentative Statements	_____	or	_____
9. Expresses Views Readily	_____	or	_____
10. Waits to be Introduced	_____	or	_____

(Answers to "Direct or Indirect?": Odd numbers - Direct; Even numbers - Indirect)

Open or Guarded?

	Open		Guarded
1. Animated Facial Expressions	_____	or	_____
2. Expects Other to Arrive on Time	_____	or	_____
3. Tells Stories and Anecdotes	_____	or	_____
4. Conversations Focused on Tasks	_____	or	_____
5. Shares Personal Feelings Easily	_____	or	_____
6. More Formal, Proper Style and Dress	_____	or	_____
7. Asks How You Feel About Things	_____	or	_____
8. Poker-Faced, Does Not Smile Easily	_____	or	_____
9. Comfortable with Touching	_____	or	_____
10. Want to See Evidence	_____	or	_____

(Answers to "Open or Guarded?": Odd numbers - Open; Even numbers - Guarded)

SECTION III

ADAPTABILITY STRATEGIES FOR HOTEL SALESPEOPLE

"Knowledge without application is useless."

Many of us have all heard that age-old axiom. Understanding your natural behavioral style and learning to recognize another person's style is a good start to sales success. Yet unless you are willing and able to adapt, you have gained nothing. This section will teach you how to make adjustments in your approach to others to reduce tension and engender trust.

CHAPTER 7

BEHAVIORAL ADAPTABILITY

willingness to develop and demonstrate behaviors not necessarily characteristic of your own style, for the benefit of every relationship, is called "behavioral adaptability." This type of flexibility is applied more to you to your patterns, attitudes, and habits than those of others. Behavioral adaptability involves making intentional adjustments to your methods of communicating and behaving, based on the particular needs of the relationship at a specific moment in time.

Behavioral adaptability is the key to successfully communicating your ideas to people of every style.

As you continue to develop more adaptability, you will more effectively interact with each person in the way he or she likes to communicate, learn, and make purchases.

Adapting your behavioral style is a major change; such big changes take time. Here is a simple test: move an appliance you use every day (toaster, coffee maker, electric razor, etc…) before going to bed. Quite likely, when you wake up in the morning and go to make toast, coffee or shave, you will automatically go to where the appliance used to be as opposed to its new location. Although old habits are hard to break some are worth breaking!

It's not easy to break the old habit of "selling the way you buy." You need to learn to sell to people based on their style, learning to alter your sales strategies and techniques to fit four different buying styles.

To date, you have been interacting with other people in a way that "works" for you. Feedback from your parents, siblings, relatives, teachers, and friends shaped your psyche. You will require practice and focus to "unlearn" reflexive communication modes and to develop new reactions to situations and people.

The beauty of our sales technique is that, unlike traditional sales training, you learn more than just "selling techniques." You learn to read the behavioral styles of others and adjust your selling style to one that best fits their buying style. If you are a jokester or storyteller (Socializer), you will learn when and how to use your natural gifts at a more appropriate time to get the results you want. Additionally, you can also learn how to use your agile, creative mind to ask better questions of your customers to gain valuable information and/or solidify your relationship.

The first few times you consciously adapt your style to mesh with others, the result will be awkward. Like trying anything new for the first time, it takes practice. But with enough practice you will eventually find it easy to read the style of others for the purpose of matching your selling style to that of the customer's preferred buying style. That will be the magic moment in time when you begin to benefit from increased sales, and indirectly benefit by having a better relationship with your colleagues, friends, relatives, and family members.

No one style is naturally more adaptable than another is. For a given situation, the appropriate adjustments that people of each behavioral style needs to make will vary. The decision to employ specific behaviors is made on a case-by-case, situational basis. For instance, you may have to be flexible with one person and less flexible with another. You may want to be quite flexible with one person today and less flexible with that same individual tomorrow. Behavioral adaptability concerns the way you manage your communication and action strategies.

For example, when a Socializer meets with a Thinker, one of the ways the Socializer can practice behavioral adaptability is by talking less, listening more, and focusing on the key facts. This is not being disingenuous; it simply means that the Socializer makes an effort to put the Thinker's priorities ahead of his own, knowing that both their needs will eventually be met.

Adaptability does not mean imitating the other person's behavioral style. It means adjusting your Directness/Indirectness and Openness/Guardedness (your pace and priority) with the other person in ways that lead to synergy and better outcomes for both of you. It means you can make these adjustments while maintaining your own identity, ideas and good business sense.

Adaptability is important to successful relationships of all kinds. People may display a different style to meet the requirements of their professional roles than what they prefer in their social and/or personal lives. Interestingly, people tend to be more adaptable at work with people they know little about, while being less adaptable at home with people they know well. People who maintain high adaptability in all situations have difficulty coping with stress or realistic requirements for efficiency. There is also the danger of developing tension from the stress of remaining in a "foreign" style permanently rather than as a temporary, more situational response. At the other end of the continuum, little or no behavioral adaptability will cause others to view people as a rigid and uncompromising "robot" because they insist on behaving according to only their own natural pace and priority. Of course, adaptation at its extreme could make you appear two-faced.

High adaptors meet the needs of others as well as their own. Through attention and practice, they are able to achieve a balance, intentionally using their flexibility by recognizing when a modest accommodation is appropriate or when the nature of the situation calls for them to completely adapt to the other person's behavioral style. Skilled adaptors know how to negotiate relationships in a way that allows everyone to win. They are tactful, reasonable, understanding, and non-judgmental.

Your adaptive level influences how others judge their relationship with you. When you raise your adaptive level, both trust and credibility will rise in the eyes of customers. Adaptability even enables you to interact more productively with difficult people and respond better to tense or complex situations. By adapting, you are truly practicing **The Platinum Rule** by treating the other person the way they want to be treated.

Once you understand your own primary style and the style of the person with whom you want to build rapport, you can begin to adapt your style. Your first adaptations should be *pace* and *priority*. By making simple adjustments in your speed of operation and your focus on tasks or relationships, you can eliminate a great deal of relationship "static." Remember that changing your style takes time, practice, and patience. This is a process that is not a quick fix but worth the effort. From this point forward, consider every human interaction a wonderful opportunity to practice raising your level of adaptation to increase your sales performance and enhance the quality of your personal life.

PACE AND PRIORITY

There are two primary areas of difference that cause static and/or tension when communicating with others – pace and priority. Pace is a person's operating speed. Some people prefer a faster, high-energy pace, while others prefer to operate more slowly. Priority is what the person sees as most important, their natural inner goal or drive. It is a natural focus on either the tasks and results or relationships and feelings.

You may remember that a primary quality that distinguishes Direct from Indirect people is their pace. Direct people tend to move, think, talk, and make decisions rapidly; Indirect people move more slowly.

Another major factor that differentiates Open and Guarded people is their priorities. Open people tend to place a higher priority on interpersonal relationships while those who are Guarded view working on tasks as their priority. Each style has a unique set of priorities involving the type of relationship or task that is important to them, and each has its own pace in terms of how fast things should be done. The remainder of this chapter will help you develop specific strategies for adjusting your pace and priority to meet the needs of other people within all of your relationships.

Adjusting Your Pace

If you are a Direct person, you tend to operate at a fast rate. If you want to connect with an Indirect person, you will want to talk, walk, and make decisions with them more slowly. Seek the opinions of the other person and find ways to acknowledge their ideas. Invite the person to share in the decision-making process and follow their lead rather than trying to take control. Try to relax and be a little calmer.

Engage in active listening to ensure that you thoroughly understand what the other person is saying. Resist your impulses to interrupt; if necessary, jot down one or two-word notes to remind you about your ideas later. Listen more than you talk and, while you are speaking, provide pauses to encourage the other person to speak. Avoid the impulse to criticize, challenge, or push the communication along faster than the other person. Try to find points of agreement, but if you do disagree, choose your words carefully and do not intimidate the Indirect person.

By contrast, if you are an Indirect person, you tend to operate at a slower speed. If you are dealing with a Direct person, you will want to talk, walk and make decisions with them more rapidly. Initiate conversations and give recommendations. Use direct statements and avoid tentative, roundabout questions. Communicate with a strong, confident voice and maintain eye contact. If you disagree with the Direct person, express your opinion confidently but tactfully. Face the conflict openly without turning the conflict into a personal attack.

Adjusting Your Priority

If you are an Open person, relationships and feelings primarily motivate you; they are your top priority. If you are dealing with a Guarded person whose top priority is getting things done, you must make a behavioral adjustment. Increase your task-oriented focus by getting right to the agenda. Talk about and focus on the bottom line of the project at hand. The person you are dealing with will want logic and facts; so be prepared to provide proof of your rationale with supporting information.

Consider finding a Guarded associate to help you review your presentation or proposal for logic and flow of information. Prepare an agenda of what items to include in your meeting and try to adhere to that agenda. Avoid getting frustrated if you find yourself getting off-track, the agenda will enable you to refocus on the task. When you have completed the agenda, end the meeting on a cordial, but businesslike note.

Guarded people do not like to be touched by strangers or to have their physical space invaded. Do not initiate physical contact until you are sure it will be positively received. Downplay your natural enthusiasm and body movement; a Guarded person often views an excess of enthusiasm as "hype." It's much better to have a well-developed, logical presentation based on factual information. Dress and speak in a professional manner compatible with the successful people in your industry. A Guarded person needs to trust and respect you and your credibility.

If you are a Guarded person interacting with an Open person, remember to develop the relationship first. Share some of your feelings. Let your emotions show and let the Open person know who you are and what you like. Observe the other person's environment and find a picture, trophy, art object, or something else you have in common, then ask him/her questions about that object. Try to find out what interests the Open person. Find something about the person or the person's environment that you can sincerely compliment.

Listen and respond to expressions of feelings. Find out what it takes to make the Open person look good within his organization. Take the time to develop a strong relationship based on your understanding of his needs and objectives. Use friendly language and communicate more fully. Be flexible with your agenda and be willing to address the interests of the Open person rather than your own.

In time, adjusting your pace and priority to that of the customer's will become natural to you. You will not have to think your way through adapting with others, it will flow subconsciously. And salespeople may expect four key payoffs for investing efforts at becoming more adaptable to the behavioral style of customers. Those who develop their adaptability skills are likely to become more:

1. **Successful:** remember the common bond among successful people is their ability to establish and maintain rapport with customers

2. **Effective:** as you are able to develop better working relationships with people, you will dramatically increase your personal productivity

3. **Satisfied:** strong, meaningful relationships add a deeply satisfying aspect to our lives

4. **Fulfilled:** fulfill your dreams and goals with the help and support of those around you

SECTION IV

EASY 5 STEP SELLING PROCESS

We have finally arrived at the point of the book where the knowledge gained on reading the behavioral styles of others will transform the way you do hotel sales forever. Our easy five step selling process of connecting, exploring, collaborating, confirming and assuring will be first be described. Then you will learn how to adapt the way you sell to the four behavioral styles using those five steps to increase the odds of booking business for your hotel.

CHAPTER 8

ADAPTING THE SALES PROCESS
TO THE FOUR STYLES

The five definable steps in our selling process are listed below. Successfully guiding the four behavioral styles through each step will increase the likelihood of a sale.

Step 1. Connecting: This is the first critical step that begins the process of learning the style of the customer and adapting one's selling style to increase the possibility of making a sale. When customers learn that salespeople sincerely have their interests at heart, the rest of the sales process continues with fewer obstacles. Once customers begin to trust you, they will feel more comfortable about sharing their business goals, challenges, and shortcomings.

Step 2. Exploring: Discovering the needs and wants of the customer is the number one priority for successful hotel salespeople. They explore the customer's situation for needs, opportunities, and ideas about how to help move them toward achieving goals or solving problems.

Step 3. Collaborating: In this step, salespeople get their customers involved in the process of booking a piece of business. They collaborate heavily in this step to ensure the hotel meets the needs and expectations of customers.

Step 4. Confirming: Gaining a firm commitment from a customer at this point in the selling cycle is often a formality if the first three steps were handled properly. Yet this stage is a critical part of solidifying a partnership between hotel salespeople and their customers to meet the needs and expectations of both parties.

Step 5. Assuring: Assuring customer satisfaction is the last step of our sales process; it is key to long-term, extraordinary success in selling. Although many salespeople pay little or no attention to their customers after they book the business, the most successful salespeople are the ones who are always there to make sure the customer was completely satisfied with the services it provided to customers through constructive feedback.

STEP 1

Connecting: Establishing Rapport

The purpose of making contact with your customer is to begin opening lines of communication. Professional salespeople know that a solid business association goes beyond the immediate product or service offered; it is based on the relationship built over time between hotel salespeople and customers. When customers know salespeople sincerely have their best interests in mind, the rest of the sales process can continue because they appreciate salespeople who show an interest in helping them solve problems and achieve their goals.

You can make contact with customers three ways: face-to-face, via the telephone, or by letter of introduction. Each makes a different impression and has its advantages and disadvantages. While face-to-face meetings make the strongest impression, they are also the most time consuming and costly. Each sales situation dictates a different mix of contact types to maximize effectiveness.

Prior to actually connecting with the customer to determine his or her style you might consider speaking to someone who knows him or her prior to connecting so you are ready to adapt to that person's style when first meeting on the phone or in person. When speaking to someone in the company who knows the customer you have set up a meeting with at the hotel or their office, you might ask some of the following questions:

1. "Is _____ a real 'take charge' kind of boss, or is she more 'easy going?'"

2. "In meetings, does _____ do a lot of the talking, or does she usually sit back and listen to the opinions of other team members?"

3. "Does _____ like to discuss politics, news, weather or family… general chitchat, or is she a 'let's-stick-to-the-business-at-hand' kind of person?"

4. "Would you consider _____ to be a swift decision maker, or does she often weigh many options before proceeding?"

The answers to these four questions will give you a good snapshot of the customer's behavioral style. This information will be invaluable to you when preparing to meet the customer for the first time because you will already have an idea of their behavioral style and prepare yourself accordingly.

If your first contact is over the telephone, you can still determine a customer's style by listening attentively. Note their rate of speech, the evenness or variations in tone, and overall demeanor. Also, be aware of how much they try to direct and/or control the conversation. Directors will often come across as impatient, terse and cool. Socializers will interrupt you often, talk more than they listen and seem very animated and persuasive. Relaters will listen carefully, allow the conversation to drift, and will not notice the passage of time. Thinkers will also listen well, but they will be more formal and less free with your use of their time.

The introductory face-to-face meeting with your customer is the first critical test. Your understanding of behavioral styles, body language (image), your listening and questioning skills, and your knowledge of the hotel will have an impact on the impression you make in the first few minutes of a meeting. In that short, precious time, you can make or break the sale because the customer will determine whether or not they want to do business with your hotel.

Regardless of the style of any customer, every person you encounter will respond positively to an attentive, patient and intelligent listener. The best way to build rapport with anyone is to ask interesting questions and aggressively listen to responses. Unfortunately, we strive to improve how we present our ideas, but rarely do we learn how to listen and connect with others.

The two most important skills for successful hotel salespeople are observing the behavior of customers, and LISTENING! Not superficial listening where the salesperson is taught to "always be closing," but really engaging in active listening to determine the behavioral style of the customer and then adapting the sales process to accommodate that style.

Active listening is unquestionably the most comprehensive, and potentially powerful, level of listening. It best fits with behavioral adaptability in a given range of varied situations. Although demanding and tiring, active listening requires the deepest level of concentration, attention, mental, and emotional processing effort.

This most active type of listener refrains from coming to judgment about the customer's message, focusing instead on understanding his/her point of view. The focus is on the thoughts, intentions and feelings of the customer, as well as the spoken words. Listening in this manner requires the suspension of personal thoughts, feelings, and biases. It also requires that the listener sends verbal and nonverbal feedback to the speaker, indicating that what is being said is really being absorbed and truly understood.

Take notes. Do not trust your memory when data and facts are important; use phrases and key words to record the pros and cons of positions, impressions, and questions that enter into your mind. Do not attempt to take minutes of the meeting or record complete reactions. Ask the other's permission before taking notes and come prepared with your own pad and pen.

Listen "between the words." What is said may not be what the person means. Learn to read the subtle and not-so-subtle signals that speak so honestly.

Be alert to shifts. Everyone has a unique way of expressing attitude changes. The words may continue, but changes in eye contact, vocal tone, speaking pace, posture, and facial expression may indicate feelings the words are not communicating.

Great listeners make the best salespeople. Master the skill of effective listening and personal relationships may improve with family and friends, too. As important as listening skills are, it is equally important to communicate the features and benefits of your hotel in a manner that resonates with the customer's behavioral style.

Step 2

Exploring: Asking Smart Questions

The purpose of Exploring is to get information: an accurate picture of the customer's needs and what it will take to provide an effective solution. To do so, we need to listen to what the customer says, but we also need to know how to ask the right questions to get the relevant information.

Asking intelligent questions is a critical sales skill. It does not require asking many questions but the right ones. The art of questioning is the cornerstone of exploring the customer's needs. It is paramount to a successful career in sales. Asking questions is similar to painting a picture. We start with a blank canvas and begin to fill in the background and rough in the picture with broad-brush strokes. Then we fill in the details using increasingly finer strokes.

With questioning, we start with broad strokes asking the customer broad, open questions that rough in a lot of his situation. "Tell me about your business" not only starts to give you information about your customer's situation; it gives them a chance to relax and tell you what they think is important. If you start with a smaller brush, "How many room nights did you book last year?" that's an okay question. Yet sales may not be what customer's primary concern right now.

Broad, open-ended questions show your interest in the customer's situation. They often start with "Tell me ...," "how," "what," "why." "How do you see our hotel help you to achieve the goals of your business conference?" "What amenities do you think will be most valuable to your attendees?" "What questions do you have that I have not addressed to this point?" They are much more powerful than closed-ended questions that require a simple yes or no answer or specific information.

Of course, salespeople use closed questions when they need specific decisions to be make, such as "How many people do you expect to attend your high school reunion?" It is important to understand when to use each type. Once you have started the questioning process, you want to build the responses you have received. You are following the lead of your customer. This is commonly referred to as a "funnel" or "channeling" technique of questioning… you start with broad, open questions such as, "Tell me the mission statement of your new product launch exposition?"

Keep in mind that your opening question will be very important in creating a good impression with your prospect because it has to match the behavioral style of the customer. There are major benefits to asking such a broad question as, "Could you tell me a little about your business?" A question like that gives customers complete freedom to answer in any way they choose. This has a relaxing effect. It also helps to determine the customer's behavioral style, and you will adjust your follow up questions accordingly. Lastly, the answer to this question may reveal needs and opportunities. If it does not, they will become apparent as you build subsequent questions around this answer.

STEP 3

The Collaborating Step: Maintaining Rapport

The purpose of the Exploring step of the sale was to uncover the needs and expectations of the customer once the goals and expectations of the event have been determined. In this step, the salesperson Collaborates with the customer to finalize all the details of the event if a room block is required, if meeting rooms will be needed, if there is to be food and beverage functions, and so forth. It's the process of taking the customer's ideas and integrating them into the final contract to ensure that the hotel can meet the needs and expectations of the customer. It is critical to flesh out all the customer's needs and expectations at this stage so that there are absolutely no unpleasant surprises to either party after the contract has been signed.

The give-and-take exchange can be thought of as an opportunity to "switch places" with the customer. Imagine telling the customers: "If you and I could switch places, what questions remain that have not been addressed to ensure that the event is a complete success?" That's the ultimate; to come as close as possible to the perfect knowledge that would allow the salesperson to plan a perfect meeting or event for the customer. This cannot happen unless the customers are forthcoming on their needs and expectations and the hotel can absolutely deliver on all that was promised in the contract.

The primary roadblock to such a thorough exchange of information is time. There simply is not enough of it. Keep in mind the "three T's" of information exchange: Time, Trust, and Tension. If you decrease tension and build trust, the customer will want to spend more time with you.

Speaking the Language of Benefits

Successful hotel salespeople know how to speak the language of benefits rather than features. A feature is some aspect of the whole product that exists regardless of a customer's needs. A benefit is the way that features satisfy a customer need. A benefit is a feature in action.

Most customers think in terms of benefits. They do not care how something works; they want to know what it will do for them or how it will solve their problems. The bottom-line benefit is what the key decision seeks using the pace and priority that matches the behavioral style of the customer.

One way to get customers involved in the collaboration stage is to use the feature-feedback-benefit (FFB) method. A feature is presented with a question that asks for customer feedback. For instance, a hotel salesperson might say, "This ballroom can be divided into four smaller meeting spaces. How important would that be to your conference to use it for the opening general sessions and then smaller breakout sessions on the first day of the conference?" That begins a discussion about the functionality of the hotels meeting space. If it is not an important benefit, you can go on to the next feature until you find the most pressing needs of the customer. Other open-ended information questions that are effective during this stage are:

"How do you see our renovated breakout rooms fitting in with your education conference?"

"How might the fitness center and spa be a benefit to your business meeting?"

"How do you see the outdoor patio accommodating your wedding party?"

"Is there anything about the hotel that does not appear to meet the needs of your group compared to other hotels you have toured?"

"What concerns do you have about our attrition policy for unsold rooms in your room block?"

STEP 4

Confirming Stage: Maintaining Rapport

Gaining the customer's commitment flows naturally out of the Exploring and Collaborating stages for the successful hotel salesperson. Doing a good job during the first three steps of our sales process makes it easier to book the business. In fact, a study by Forum Corporation showed that the top sales professionals – the superstars – seldom use a closing technique. In approximately 46% of their sales, they never had to ask for a commitment. When they do ask, it is usually no more than a nudge along the lines of, "Any reason why we shouldn't move forward?"

Top salespeople stay in sync with their customers, taking each step one-at-a-time. Once the first three steps have been completed, signing the contract should be a formality. However, gaining true commitment from a customer should not be as simple as closing the deal and signing the contract. The goal of successful salespeople is to develop a loyal customer instead of "making a sale."

The Confirming stage is a critical point in building a customer partnership. Top salespeople know how to use acceptance, rejection, or even postponement to develop stronger ties with their customers. They never stoop to using the Ben Franklin close, trial close, standing-room-only, or any other traditional sales closing techniques to earn a piece of business, either. The sales method they use is a very natural process of two or more people sharing information to develop a solution to a problem or need. It requires trust, respect, and open communication on both sides. You cannot work through all the stages of the sale and then, at the end, try to use a manipulative closing technique to clinch the deal. It does not make sense because it does not work.

In traditional selling, the salespeople ask "closed" questions frequently meant to force the customer to buy, such as the forced-choice close, the sharp angle close, closing on the final objection, or the "I want to think it over" close. Here is where the salespeople really try to take total control of the sales situation and the customer. However, this is where the customers really have the strongest need to gain what they want. They can best do so by retaining their inherent right to make this decision without being railroaded into a decision by the salesperson even if it was the decision they were already going to make.

This creates problems in the sales relationship. Often, the customer may create smokescreens as a defense mechanism to ward off the salesperson. A smokescreen is something that clouds the relationship or obscures the decision-making process. Common smokescreens are "Your price is too high," and "I want to think about it" or "I'll get back to you." These statements indicate that the customer is uncomfortable communicating uncertainty, avoiding telling their true feelings and thoughts. What they are not telling you are their true concerns.

Dealing with Customer Concerns

In the traditional sales training model, salespeople learn techniques to help them overcome objections. Nothing is more frustrating than to work hard exploring customer needs and collaborating on creative solutions to their problems only to have them object at the last minute.

Successful hotel salespeople have learned to change their terminology. For example, they drop the word "objections" and call them "customer concerns." Talking about objections makes it sound like customers are being difficult. They are not being difficult; they are expressing concerns about some aspect of the hotels amenities (no matter how big or small), or ability to pull off the event as proposed.

The best way to end the "objection" situation is to avoid it in the first place. If the salesperson does his/her due diligence and gathers sufficient information from the first three steps, collaborating with the customer along the way, there should be no real objections to booking the business with your hotel in the Commitment step of the five step selling process.

If the customer has a problem booking their business at your hotel, it should have been identified long before getting to the Commitment step. The salesperson and customer can then shake hands early on and agree the hotel might not work for the current piece of business, but agree to consider it for future business.

Part of dealing with customers' concerns is to move past any discontentment they may have and welcome the opportunity to better understand the needs and expectations of customers. Rather than being viewed as rejections, these concerns are course corrections. Customers are often reluctant to express their real concerns up-front; sometimes they surface at the Connecting step of the selling cycle. Perhaps the salesperson did not adapt to the behavioral style of the customer; perhaps the customer did not have a good feeling about the property after the site visit, compared to the other hotels they toured. But the salesperson should work hard to identify the customers concerns early on so that time is not wasting pursuing a piece of business that has already been awarded to another hotel in the customer's head.

Customer concerns should not be viewed as a roadblock as much as an opportunity to explain how the hotel will meet their needs and expectations. Here are four steps to help you effectively deal with customer concerns at the Commitment step of the selling cycle:

Listen: Hear the customer out. Listen carefully for clues to help you discover their true concern. Sometimes salespeople lose potential sales trying to jump in too soon and overcome an objection. Remember to hear out the concern completely prior to responding.

Clarify: Ask questions to make sure you have a complete understanding of the concern from the customer point of view. What do customers mean when they say the price is too high, they need to think about it, or they need to talk to a friend?

Respond: Respond appropriately to the concern. Refer back to the decision criteria established in the Exploring step and make sure that each point is still valid. Review the features and benefits of your property to see where each criterion applies and where it is not measuring up.

Confirm: Make sure the customer is satisfied with the hotels ability to satisfy a specific need or want. The salesperson does not want it to surface again as the time to sign the contract approaches.

The way salespeople respond to customer concerns depends on the type of customer concern and the selling step. Each step of the selling cycle has different types of customer concerns. In the beginning, most are simply "put-offs." The customer is really dissatisfied with the hotel after the site visit and does not want to sit and work out a contract. They have chosen another hotel and not going to tell you. In the later steps, customers may object to the proposed cost of booking their business at your hotel, or discover that the property is deficient in certain amenities once the details of the event are being worked out.

Losing the sale at the Commitment step may simply be the case of not adapting to the behavioral style of the customer in the Connecting step. Reading and adapting to the behavioral style of the customer is the foundation of our selling process. If the relationship collapses at the Connecting step, so does everything it supports. This happens because trust was broken; the selling style of the salesperson did not match that of the customer creating tension between the two shaking the confidence of the customer. Whatever the cause for the style mismatch, the salesperson needs to use all of his/her communication skills to get the relationship back on track.

STEP 5

Assuring Stage: Cementing Rapport

The greatest weakness of most salespeople is the way they handle the Assuring step of the sales process. Once they have sold the client on booking business with the hotel, they hand it over to those in the hotel who will be responsible for honoring the terms of the signed contract, and move on to the next prospect!

Anybody who knows about the lifetime value of a customer does not need to be reminded of how important it is to make sure they are available to those in the functional areas of the hotel who might have questions about the terms of the contract, as well as follow-up with the customer during and after their stay to make sure the contract was executed as agreed! Customers need the chance to tell salespeople whether they are 100% satisfied with the quality of service provided by the hotel – and feel comfortable telling the salesperson where the hotel did not meet their needs and expectations. The salesperson then needs to be in a position to do more than apologize for mistakes made by the hotel and take action by offering a refund or offer other tangible ways to incentivize the customer to consider the property for future business. Once customers lose confidence in the hotels ability to deliver on their future needs and expectations it will terminate the business relationship.

Assuring customer satisfaction is a critical ingredient of extraordinary sales success. Salespeople benefit from assuring customers in two ways. First of all, it increases the probability of repeat business. Customers will give future business to those salespeople who met their needs and expectations, especially when the salesperson follows up to see how a future event can be managed even better in the future.

Secondly, dissatisfied customers can now turn to social media to share their bad experiences with thousands of prospective customers like Yelp!, Trip Advisor, the hotel's Facebook page. Customers are especially talkative when they get bad service. Before the advent of the Internet, customers told up to 20 others about their bad experience. Today's customers can literally reach thousands, if not millions, of prospective customers as they share the poor service received at your hotel.

Getting Customer Feedback

The process of getting customer feedback after the conclusion of their event begins with a hand-written, "thank you" note. It is amazing how many salespeople still overlook this simple step. Try it for a while and see how many of your customers mention it, or display it somewhere in their office.

The next follow-up may come one to two weeks later to make sure the event truly went as planned. It may involve an online survey or personal telephone call, or both. This gives the salesperson the chance to reconnect with customers and learn what went right or what went wrong with the event that was not communicated while it was taking place at the hotel, for whatever reason. It is also not a bad time to ask the customer for the opportunity to win future business, albeit rooms, food & beverage functions, and/or events and meetings at the hotel. No matter the customer, or the nature of the event held at your hotel, a phone call thanking them for their business is appreciated by all of the behavioral styles. Especially when the "thank you" is in the form that would be most appreciated by the behavioral style of the customer.

The power of calling customers and thanking them for their business is evidenced by a sales blitz that was conducted by students enrolled in Dr. La Lopa's sales class for a Marriott property. The students in the sales class are required to do a sales blitz for a hotel to get hands-on sales experience. They typically go to the hotel the night before the blitz where they are greeted by the salespeople in an opening reception and given an orientation and tour to prepare them for the blitz. On the day of the blitz they typically call or go visit previous customers to confirm contact information and asking if they may have any business coming up in the future that the hotel could service. Such was not the case for this blitz. All the students were asked to do was call previous customers and simply "Thank You" for their business. That was it. Amazingly, the hotel generated tens of thousands of dollars in hot leads without asking for any future business.

CHAPTER 9

Adapting to Directors

General Strategy: Be Efficient and Competent

When adapting your style to Directors, acknowledge what is most important to them. Prioritize their goals and then let them know how you can be an asset for helping them achieve each one. Be professional and competent. Get down to business immediately. Be punctual or early to the appointment, have a prepared agenda and adhere to it! If you find yourself running late for the meeting, be sure to call ahead and explain the reasons for your tardiness, apologize, and give the Director the option either to move ahead with the meeting as planned or to reschedule. Of course, calling to apologize for tardiness is merely a common courtesy for all of the behavioral styles, but it is critical to do so with people who place a high value on their time.

Give Directors two to three of the best options and offer a succinct analysis of each to help them make a decision. Be brief, efficient and thoroughly prepared. Directors want to know what your hotel can do for them and what it will cost. They are interested in saving time, bottom-line results, increasing profitability, and moving forward to gain an edge over the competition. If you disagree with them, keep your differences based on facts rather than personal feelings.

Step 1: Connecting

Directors want you to get right to the point, so just give them enough information to satisfy their need to know about your hotel's competence to handle their piece of business. They do not want you to waste their time giving them a bolt-by-bolt description of your hotel meeting space, presenting a long list of testimonials from satisfied customers, or getting too chummy with them—always remember that they are Direct and Guarded. When you write, call, or meet a Director, do it in a formal, businesslike manner. Refer to bottom line results, increased efficiency, saved time, return on investment, profits, and so on. In other words, tell him what's in it for him. Take care to be well organized, time-conscious, efficient and businesslike. They do not want to make friends with you; they want to get something out of you if they think you have something of value to offer. In other words, tell Directors what they will gain by booking a piece of business with your hotel.

When making a sales presentation to Directors, be sure to move at a quicker pace as they are frustrated with a slower pace. Directors become especially wary if they are unsure about a salesperson's competence. Make sure they do not question yours! Remember, Directors do not want to make friends with salespeople; they want to do business with hotel salespeople who are extremely competent.

The goal is to provide sufficient information and incentive for the Director to do business with your hotel. When you call, you might say, "Some of the ways I thought our hotel could host your event are x, y, z; could we schedule a meeting to address those options at the time of your choosing?" By piquing the curiosity of Directors, they may agree to a meeting unless, of course, they are not interested. Since Directors pride themselves in being busy, they dislike granting several meetings, but if they think meeting with you will save time and money, they are likely to explore your proposal.

Step 2: Exploring

To avoid Director's impatience before it surfaces, keep your conversations interesting by alternately asking questions and offering relevant information. Directors need to view the meeting as purposeful; so they want to understand where your questions ultimately lead. When asking questions, fine-tune and make them as practical and logical as possible. Aim questions at the heart of the issue and ask them in a straightforward manner. Only request information about their business that is unavailable elsewhere or your competence and preparation may be questioned.

When gathering information, ask questions showing you have done your homework about their industry and company. Be sure to make queries that allow them to talk about the goals of their event. Gear your information gathering toward determining how your hotel will meet all of the concerns, needs, and expectations the Director has regarding the potential event within their budget.

Step 3: Collaborating

Your proposal, whether it is combined with the exploring stage or given on its own, must be geared toward the Director's priorities (which should have been identified in the previous step). Your proposal must demonstrate how your hotel will produce the results the Director is looking for, no matter the size and scope of the business, albeit a business luncheon or a full scale conference.

Because of their lack of time, Directors do not focus as much energy contemplating and evaluating ideas. They want you to do the analysis and lay it out for them to approve or disapprove. Directors like rapid, concise analyses of their needs and your solutions.

Thus, how can hotel salespeople establish a business relationship with a Director? By being professional and prepared to address all concerns Directors have at this step of the sales process. In addition, demonstrate your competence by showing them how your hotel will help them achieve their business goals. Focus on results and highlight important specifics. Omit intermediate steps when you make your presentation, eliminate small talk, and stick to the business at hand.

Be sure to determine if Directors have any questions about the features and benefits offered by your property. You can bet that they reviewed the information in great detail before the meeting and that your hotel is in play for their event or there would be no meeting. If possible, rate the features and benefits of your hotel and explain how it measures up against the competition. Prestigious awards and honors earned by the hotel may also help Directors give you their business because it will make them look good.

Providing Directors printed and digital information about the features and benefits of your hotel is one thing. Hotel salespeople must have all those facts and figures in their head when the Director starts to fire off questions at a seemingly faster-than-the-speed-of-mouth rate. The Director already knows the answers to many of their questions; they are designed to test the competence of the hotel salesperson. Having to refer back to the marketing materials, or answer a question with uncertainty, will shake the confidence of the Director and possibly cost you the business.

Directors are very big on being in control, so give them choices backed with enough data and analysis to allow them to make an intelligent decision. *Then, be quiet and let them make the decision. If you speak or interrupt while they are buying, you will dramatically decrease the odds of making this sale.*

Step 4: Confirming Commitments

With Directors, you can directly ask for their business. You might say, "Based on what we've just discussed, have you decided to have your business meeting at our hotel?" Directors will often tell you "yes" or "no" with certainty. At times, Directors may appear unable to make a final decision about awarding the business to your hotel. They may not be thinking about it because they are now preoccupied with other business matters and may have put your proposal on hold.

When you draw up the contract, be careful not to spend too much time on points the Director deemed a low priority in the Collaboration step. Explain your commitment to attain both their bottom line results and your goals for a mutually acceptable agreement.

Consequently, the best way to deal with Directors is to present them with options and probable outcomes. Directors like to balance quality with cost considerations so include this information when you want them to make a decision. Offer options with supporting evidence of each option and leave the final decision to them. Directors seek control so always let them make the final decision.

While Directors are reviewing your proposal, do not keep checking back to ask if they are ready to sign a contract. They will let you know when (if) they are ready. Under no circumstance are you to make any decisions for Directors. That is the quickest way to be shown the door – no sale!

Step 5: Assuring Customer Satisfaction

The pre-con meeting is vitally important when providing event and meeting services for Directors or any piece of business for that matter – they want to know exactly who is responsible for executing the details of the contract. Because they are control freaks, they need to feel confident that those handling the details of the event are competent to do so or they will declare themselves the meeting planner to make sure things are handled correctly. That is why it is important to let Directors know the credentials of those working the event or their years of experience handling functions for the hotel.

While the event is under way, it is important to be at the beckoned call of Directors if problems arise (as they always do). Be prepared to address and resolve them on the spot to their satisfaction. If Directors do not bring problems to your attention during the event, it does not mean there were none. They may be keeping them to themselves while seething inside. You will not have to reach out to them after the event to find out if there were problems; you will be the first person they call to vent their dissatisfaction. Be prepared to listen intently to the nature of their complaint and then seek their advice on what the hotel can do to make up for it. Directors may not want a tangible solution (e.g., rebate, free room nights), they may simply want to make sure you understand how dissatisfied they were with a problem that occurred. Leave the decision up to the Director on what can be done to fix the problem and do it quickly (if it is within reason). In doing so, you will have impressed the Director by honoring your commitment to make sure the event was a success. Otherwise, they will share their disappointment with others, costing your hotel their business too.

Hotel salespeople are advised to check back periodically to make sure Directors are still happy with the way the problems were resolved. A quick phone call to check with them after the thank you note was sent is all that it takes. It will demonstrate that you care and increase the probability of earning future business.

CHAPTER 10

ADAPTING TO SOCIALIZERS

GENERAL STRATEGY: BE INTERESTED IN SOCIALIZERS

When adapting to Socializers, it is important to support their opinions, ideas, and dreams. Take the initiative by introducing yourself in a friendly, informal manner. Find out what they are trying to accomplish and let them know how you can support them. Do not hurry conversations; allow them to discuss side issues or personal interests. Be entertaining, fun, and fast moving, but do it keeping the spotlight on them and the focus on the event. Allow your animation and enthusiasm to emerge.

Clarify the specifics of any agreements in writing to make sure Socializers understand exactly what to expect from you and your hotel. Summarize who is to do what, where, and when to minimize disagreements and conflict. Use testimonials and incentives to help influence the decision process in a positive manner. Illustrate your ideas with stories and emotional descriptions that they can relate to their goals or interests.

Socializers are interested in knowing how your hotel will enhance their social status and visibility with management and meeting attendees. They are interested in saving effort, so make the process easy for them. Once they make a decision, they do not want to be bothered with excess paperwork, so you will have to draw up the contract and walk them through it. Because they prefer a minimum focus on the details, make sure they know how the hotel plans to host their event so there will be no confusion or buyer's remorse when they get the final bill.

Step 1: Connecting

Remember that Socializers are Direct and Open, so be quick-paced and focus on building the relationship as well as supporting their vision of their event. Be an especially attentive listener with Socializers. Give them positive feedback to let them know that you understand and can relate to their visions, ideas, and feelings. When you talk about yourself, your property or your meetings experience, remember to use feeling words instead of thinking words. Share your vision in emotional terms. Tell relevant humorous stories, or unusual ones, to win the heart (and sale) of Socializers. Allow them to feel comfortable by also listening to their stories, even to the point of talking about topics that may digress from the business at hand.

When you write to or personally meet with Socializers, give the letter or meeting an upbeat, friendly feeling and quick pace. Do not talk about all the features and benefits of the hotel, rather stress those aspects of your hotel that will give them what they want: the status, recognition, and joy that comes from hosting the event of the year, whether it is a birthday party or a business meeting.

The first time you call on Socializers, use a more open-ended, friendly approach. Tell them who you are and say something like, "I'd like to show you how our hotel will fit your plans to host the best New Year's Eve bash of all time!"

When you meet Socializers, try to think and feel in terms of someone who is running for election. Shake hands firmly, introduce yourself with confidence, and immediately show interest in them personally. Let them set the pace and direction of the conversation. Since Socializers typically enjoy talking about themselves, ask questions about them. Ask them about how they got started in the business, but be prepared for lengthy answers. Plan to have as many meetings as necessary to build the relationship and give them flexibility they need to make a final decision. After your first visit, you may want to meet for breakfast or lunch. Placing a time limit on those two meals is easier than putting a cap on dinner.

Step 2: Exploring

Socializers get bored quickly when they are not talking about themselves. They are also easily distracted. The salesperson must remember to strike a balance between listening to their life's stories and gathering the information needed to book the business. When asking business questions, keep them brief. If you can, work these exploratory questions in with social questions. You might ask, "What is it you want your employees to remember most about your annual holiday party?" "What will be the most important amenity to those attending your wedding?" The better your relationship with Socializers, the more willing they will be to cooperate and actively engage in booking their business.

Socializers can be so open that they may tell you their life story. If you can demonstrate how your hotel will help make their meeting dreams come true, their excitement will get them one step closer to choosing your hotel over competing properties.

Step 3: Collaborating

Style is as important as substance to Socializers, so hotel salespeople must remember the old adage that "features tell and benefits sell" is true with this style. If making a sales presentation, be sure to emphasize how your hotel would increase the Socializer's prestige, image, or recognition in the eyes of people most important to them in their social or professional circles. Sales presentations need to get to the point. Socializers will get easily bored with a lengthy, detailed, PowerPoint presentation or proposal. They want both the presentation and the presenter to both entertain and inform. The role of the salesperson is to get Socializers excited about heir hotel, and then guide them through the planning process so that the event they imagine in their head will be transferred on paper in the final contract.

Support your claims with testimonials from well-known people or high-profile corporations. Socializers respond well to other people's positive experiences with your hotel. It also helps to mention other "A-listers" who have held successful events or meetings at your hotel. If your hotel was good enough for them, they will be comfortable letting your hotel handle their event too.

Think of yourself as the organizer for the less than organized Socializer to help them get what they want out of your hotel. As a bonus for the extra effort, remember that they tend to talk up or talk down their experiences. Since they have a large social network, you can ask them if they would be willing to share with others their glowing testimonials about you and your hotel. If they were satisfied with the way the hotel handled their piece of business, no matter how big or small, Socializers will give you more referrals than the other three styles combined!

Step 4: Confirming Commitments

Be open and ask Socializers, "Where do we go from here?" or "What's our next step?" Socializers are spontaneous and respond well to the bandwagon approach of "our recently renovated ballroom is in high demand right now." If they like something, they will make a purchase decision on the spot (all other things being equal). All that is left for the salesperson to do is put the agreement in writing…and consistently reinforce the Socializer's decision

Socializers dislike extensive paperwork and details, so they are likely to hesitate or even procrastinate when it comes to spending the time required to review a lengthy contract. While a handshake is usually good enough for them, you would be wise to have a written agreement prepared due to their tendency to be unclear about business details such as procedures, responsibilities, and expectations. Both of you may hear the same words, but Socializers (as optimistic people) tend to color those words in a positive light, often to their advantage. Make sure that you agree on the specifics or, later on, you can almost bet on some degree of misunderstanding and disappointment on the part of the Socializer.

When Socializers tell you a written agreement is not necessary, simply say that the hotel will not be able to move forward without it. The contract will also help the hotel make sure everyone knows what has been agreed upon to ensure the Socializers event will be as excellent as planned!

Step 5: Assuring Customer Satisfaction

Socializers frequently make purchasing decisions before they really know if it is the right choice for them. When they jump in too quickly, the probability that they may suffer buyer's remorse is higher than for the other three behavioral styles. Socializers can benefit from ongoing reminders that they have made the right decision to book their business with your hotel. If they have planned an important social or business event at your hotel, be sure to send them regular updates on how the planning is going to keep them excited.

As is the case with all of the behavioral styles, it is important to make sure the event is going as planned. They may need to be reminded about what they had planned so there will be no confusion on their part as the hotel staff executes the details of the contract. Those attending their function had better be having a good time or that will spell trouble for the hotel sales team. Do not wait for them to get ahold of you during the function; check in with them periodically throughout the event to get their "thumbs up!"

Thank you notes should express how much it was the hotel's pleasure to be of service to Socializers. It should be a fun, colorful thank you note, if possible. That extra effort will be greatly appreciated by Socializers. A follow-up phone call should be designed to recapture the fun and excitement they felt during their event assuring them that your hotel was the right choice for their function and increasing the odds of their future business.

CHAPTER 11

ADAPTING TO THINKERS

GENERAL STRATEGY: BE THOROUGH AND WELL PREPARED

Adapting to Thinkers requires careful, well-prepared reinforcement for their organized, thoughtful approach. Greet them cordially, but then proceed quickly to the task without spending time with small talk. Demonstrate your commitment and sincerity to the sales relationship through your actions rather than words. Be systematic, precise, and provide solid, tangible, factual evidence regarding any information you provide them about your horel. Be prepared to answer the detailed questions that Thinkers may ask.

Provide all the critical information, key data and documentation required by Thinkers and provide summaries and overviews to assist in their analysis. Thinkers appreciate graphs and analyses that synthesize a substantial amount of information into a concise format. Give them a well-balanced presentation of the advantages and disadvantages of your proposal, including likely consequences. Back your proposal with written guarantees that substantially reduce their risk of making an incorrect decision. The closer you can come to a risk-free decision, the more likely you are to get an approval from Thinkers.

Thinkers want to know how your hotel will specifically accommodate their particular piece of business, including minor details. They are risk avoiders; their greatest fear is that they will be embarrassed by a poor decision. Provide them with enough data and documentation to prove the value of your proposal. Give them time to think and make their choice; avoid pushing them into a hasty decision.

Step 1: Connecting

Thinkers are Indirect and Guarded, so they are precision-oriented people who want to do their jobs in the best possible manner. They also seek confirmation that they are correct, but they will not typically volunteer that need. Going about tasks more slowly, they will need plenty of time to think through the details of their event. They do not like to be pressured into make quick decisions; they need time to process the information presented by the salesperson. They operate on a level that prefers thinking words, not feeling ones, so build your credibility by remembering to think logically instead of emotionally. Focus on their level of understanding about the "what's" and "why's" of your proposal. Make sure you elicit and provide detailed, fact-based answers to their questions.

Always begin a sales presentation with an overview so they know what to expect. Show them logical proof from reliable sources that will validate the quality of the tangible and intangible services your hotel provides (i.e., awards, certificates). Unless you can verify the hotels credentials, Thinkers may not continue the process of planning their event due to uncertainty.

It is critical to speak slowly. Enunciate and economize your words. Thinkers do not care much about social interaction (beyond common courtesy and standard pleasantries), so get to the point. Avoid making small talk and speaking about yourself except to initially establish your credibility. Thinkers tend to be somewhat humble and are naturally suspicious of those who are braggadocious.

Step 2: Exploring

Thinkers often like to answer questions that reveal their expertise, so they can be very good interviewees. As long as you ask logical, fact-oriented, relevant questions, they enjoy speaking with you. Phrase your questions to help them give you the right information. Ask open and closed-ended questions that investigate the detailed plans they may have in mind for their upcoming event; those will be essential if they are to sign a contract. Most of all, invite them to state the questions, including any key reservations, they may have about your hotel or meeting expertise so they can be dealt with in a factual manner.

Keep your answers short and concise. If you do not know the answer to a question, do not fake it. Tell them you will get the answer for them from someone on your sales team that has that expertise by a certain time and then do it.

Step 3: Collaborating

Emphasize the amenities and service quality of your hotel in a logical, accurate, value-based, quality, and reliability standpoint when collaborating with Thinkers. Present obvious disadvantages openly. Make your points and then ask if they need further clarification. They dislike talk that is not supported with fact-based evidence. If the salesperson says, "Our foodservice is the best in town," there had better be the evidence to support that claim, perhaps a glowing review from a local food critic. Elicit specific feedback by asking, "So far, what are your reactions? Do you have any issues that you'd like me to clarify?" They probably do, so encourage communication.

Show thinkers how your hotel meets the specifications of their piece of business and how you and your hotel team will handle every detail with militaristic precision, whether it is a block of rooms, business lunch, or full scale conference. Present the features and benefits of your hotel in a way that shows them they will be correct in making the purchase. Base your claims on facts, specifications, and data that relate specifically to their need gaps. When you talk about prices, relate them to the specific benefits. Thinkers are very cost-conscious; therefore, you have to increase their perceived value with facts and return-on-investment data.

Of all the types, Thinkers are the most likely to see the drawbacks; so identify the potential negatives before they do. Such honesty will enhance your credibility. If you do not draw attention to the obvious disadvantages, Thinkers may view your failure to do so as a cover-up. Let them have space to assess the relative pros-and-cons of holding their event at your hotel and make the final decision on their own without closing tactics from you.

Step 4: Confirming Commitments

Provide logical options with appropriate documentation for Thinkers. Give them enough time and sufficient data to analyze their options. They are uncomfortable with snap decisions and when they say they will think about it, they really will take their time think it over! This is not a delay tactic; they make decisions in a prudent, logical, judicious manner. However, if pressured to make a decision, they may use "I'll think about it," to buy them time to think it through.

It is highly likely that Thinkers will have already done research to find out which hotel best suits their needs and expectations, which is why you have been sent an RFP in the first place. Thinkers are educated, non-emotional "shoppers." Know how your property compares to those in your competitive set in a fact-based, statistical way, so that when they meet with competitors, you know your hotel is the best choice after they have done their due diligence to arrive at a final decision.

Step 5: Assuring Customer Satisfaction

If the Thinker planned an event at your hotel, be sure to review the details of the event with Thinkers at the pre-con meeting. They will want to know you are on top of even the most minor details to be assured you will handle their event as meticulously as planned. They put a great deal of time and energy into planning an event that will go off without a hitch and want to be assured you have put in the same effort. Once the Thinker is convinced the hotel is a focused on the details of their event, they will be more at ease.

Send a thank you note that emphasizes how the hotel delivered the event promised to the Thinkers. Perhaps cite some metrics that validate that claim: such as how the hotel adhered to the agenda, attendee satisfaction scores, or that no mistakes were made providing meals to those with food allergies. Then set a specific timetable to assess the success of the event. Make yourself available to Thinkers long after for follow-up on customer satisfaction and ask for specific feedback on your product or service performance record.

Solicit tips that Thinkers may have to help make planning a future event more efficient and effective. They will have reviewed that process during and after the event and probably have some time and money saving ideas your hotel could implement. You should also ask for their ideas and opinions for how to improve the quality of your hotel's product and service offerings. When they offer you their suggestions, get back to them about how your company is incorporating their ideas into future upgrades, revisions or new products.

CHAPTER 12

ADAPTING TO RELATERS

GENERAL STRATEGY: BE WARM AND SINCERE

Adapt to Relaters by being personally interested in them. Find out about their background, their family, their interests, and share similar information about yourself. Allow them time to develop confidence in you and move along in an informal, leisurely manner. Encourage them early on to get other interested parties involved in the decision-making process (since they will anyway). Be prepared to provide information that gives them specific assurances to help them feel that the risk is low, success is high, and all needs will be taken care of as expected with minimal changes and surprises, if at all possible.

Assume that Relaters will take things personally, so minimize disagreements and conflict. Practice your active listening skills. Be sure to take notes and display your commitment to them and their objectives. Let them know how your organization works and how it stands behind your products and services.

Relaters want to know how your product or service will affect their personal circumstances. Save them any possible embarrassment by making sure all the interested parties and decision-makers are involved with the sales process from the beginning. Keep Relaters involved and emphasize the human element of your product or service. Communicate with them in a consistent, personal manner on a regular basis.

Step 1: Connecting

Concerned with maintaining stability, Relaters want to know step-by-step procedures and action plans that are likely to meet their needs. Organize your presentation: list specifics, show sequences, and provide data. If possible, outline your proposals or materials. Satisfy their need to know the facts but also elicit their personal feelings and emotions. If you continually remind yourself that they are Open (but Indirect), they will be customers for life because you will treat them the way they want to be treated with honesty, sincerity, and personal attentiveness.

Listen patiently to Relaters, projecting your sincere interest in them as individuals. Express your appreciation for their steadiness, dependability, and cooperativeness. Get to know them personally. Present yourself as non-threatening, pleasant, and friendly, but still professional. Develop trust, credibility, and friendship at a relatively casual, informal pace. Communicate with them on a regular basis… especially at the outset. Thereafter, encourage them to contact you whenever they wish.

Contacts with Relaters are best when soft, pleasant, and specific. Explain the creature comforts of your hotel as much as possible. Mention the name of the person who referred you, if applicable. Remember, you may have the best hotel in the city, but if Relaters do not like you, or sense any insincerity, they will award their business to another salesperson that they trust more than you.

Step 2: Exploring

Relaters can be excellent interviewees. Talk warmly and informally and ask non-threatening, open-ended questions that draw them out (especially around sensitive areas). Show tact in exploring their needs.

If Relaters do not have a good feeling about you and your hotel, they are not likely hurt your feelings by telling you so. Relaters may tell you what they think you want to hear, rather than what they really think to avoid confrontations, even if they are minor ones. This same reticence may apply to telling you about their dissatisfaction with hotels that have hosted their past events. Even though this is exactly what you want to hear,

Relaters may be hesitant about saying anything negative about them.

Allow for plenty of time (possibly multiple meetings) for Relaters to open up to you and reveal their innermost desires and pains. The more time you spend with a Relater exploring, the higher the odds you'll be landing them as a customer.

Step 3: Collaborating

Show how your property will stabilize, simplify, or support Relaters procedures and relationships. Clearly define their roles and goals in your suggestions, and include specific expectations of them in the planning process. Present new ideas or variations from their planned event in a non-threatening way. Provide them with the time and opportunities to adjust to any changes in the planning process. When change becomes necessary, explain why while emphasizing all the things that are remaining the same.

Design your message to impart a sense of warmth, stability, and security. Relaters need to be reassured with comments such as, "This plan will ensure that the personal needs of you and your attendees will be met. If any changes are needed, I'll personally work with you to make necessary changes to the agenda and timetables to meet the goals and objectives of your event."

Concentrate on hotel security and round-the-clock customer support so not only will they feel safe in the hotel, but they will have someone available to call (on your personal cell phone) if there is a problem. Reassure them that the hotel staff will take personal responsibility for meeting their needs and expectations. Nothing will get in the way of the staff delivering on its promise to provide a warm, safe, friendly environment for attendees to enjoy the event hosted by the hotel.

Relaters like to be shown the appropriate steps to follow, so share those with them. Involve them by asking for their input. A question such as, "Is this an important amenity for you, or are you looking for something different?" will encourage them to give you feedback about their needs and/or decision criteria.

Step 4: Confirming Commitments

Relaters are slower, deductive decision-makers. They listen to the opinions of others and take time to solicit those opinions before deciding. Provide personal guidance, direction, or assurance as required for pursuing the safest, most practical course to follow. Make a specific action plan to arm them with literature, case studies, and any documentation you have available, because they will be "selling" your proposal to other within decision influencers. Be sure not to change a single aspect of the agreement without first discussing it with Relaters, who do not like unexpected changes.

Try not to rush Relaters, but do provide gentle, helpful nudges to help them decide (when needed). Otherwise, they may postpone their decision. Involve them by personalizing the plan and showing how it will directly benefit them or those whom will be attending the event. When asking for a commitment, guide them toward a choice if they seem indecisive. Quite often, they will feel relieved that you are helping them decide.

Another approach is to take the lead with Relaters. Once you have determined which action is in their best interest, lead them to the confirmation with your recommendation. When you have gained agreement, you can gently lead Relaters to the next step. There is nothing pushy or manipulative about this if you have studied your customer's goals and pain points. You are simply recommending the best solution that you honestly believe best satisfies their personal and event needs. You have created a win-win situation. Anything less is actually a losing proposition for this customer… and for you.

Step 5: Assuring Customer Satisfaction

If the Relater has booked an event with your hotel, be sure to personally introduce him/her to all those who will be responsible for executing their event at the pre-con meeting. Let each member of your team explain how they will ensure the safety, security, and enjoyment of those attending their event. If Relaters are assured that those important to them are going to be taken care of, they will be happy with the hotel. Be sure to check in with Relaters during the event to see how they are feeling about the way the event is going. Tell them any and all potential problems are your utmost concern and sharing them will not hurt your feelings. That is how important their event is to you!

It is important to follow-up consistently with a Relater to make sure they are pleased with the service being provided by the hotel. Give them your personal guarantee that you will remain in touch, keep things running smoothly, and be available on an "as needed" basis. Relaters like to think they have a special relationship with you, that you are more than just another business acquaintance. They prefer a continuing, predictable relationship. Give them your cell number, along with an invitation to call you any time with any concern. They will rarely use it, but will feel secure knowing it's available to them. They dislike one-time deals, so follow up to maintain your relationship. Impersonal, computerized follow-up is not very appealing to Relaters, so continue building your relationship with low-key, personalized attention and assistance.

When sending a thank you note, be sure it states how it was your sincere pleasure to host the Relater's event at your hotel. Alternatively, comment on how attendees complimented your staff for doing such a good job. Plan a time convenient to Relaters to assess the success of the event in a relaxed, constructive manner.

CHAPTER 13

So, You Did Not Make the Sale. Now What?

If customers decline or delay the decision to do business with your hotel, you still have obligations to follow up to determine the reason your hotel lost the business to a competitor. Conversely, what is your track record on prompt follow-up with those who have given you their business to determine their satisfaction level with the services provided by the hotel? Is it timely or simply when you get around to it? It is not a task to be dreaded; the highest performers are eager to learn whether they met the needs and expectations of their customers...or fell short. That is the only way to improve on planning, managing, and assessing future business opportunities.

Let's take a look at the bad news first: No contract! Time for following up with those customers. First things first, customers deserve to be sincerely thanked for giving the hotel an opportunity to respond to their RFP. A hand-written note is always appreciated and sets you apart from the vast majority of salespeople who take shortcuts or move on to their next sale.

Next, you need to stop and objectively reflect upon the circumstances that caused a prospective customer to book their business with a competitor. In doing so, you may have a better chance to earn that business at a later date, or that of customers with similar styles.

Here is a list of questions you could ask yourself when debriefing a lost piece of business:

- Did they decline because I proposed a solution before fully Exploring and Collaborating?

- Did I do my best possible job of asking questions, encouraging them to share their ideas... or did I propose too many of my ideas?

- Did I adjust my style to their pace or priority?

- Did I adapt to their behavioral style to the best of my ability?

- Based on their reasoning for not selecting my RFP, what can I change in the future with this prospect and future prospects?

Truly successful hotel salespeople learn from their mistakes and do not repeat them in the future. They learn to turn a "no" into a "yes" when finding out why they did not get a particular piece of business so they are better prepared to use our five step selling process when meeting the next prospect.

Commonly, salespeople may be in the right place (a qualified customer), but at the wrong time. Prospective customers, if empowered to educate themselves over time, can (and often do) change their minds. However, prospective customers do not like to do so in front of salespeople. They may do so at a later date and that is the best reason to follow up!

There are two different types of follow-ups that you can execute, each serves a specific function. The first is a standard follow up. The salesperson sends literature, case studies, testimonials and other "value proposition" information designed to educate the customer further about the value of your hotels amenities, upcoming renovations and so forth. Sometimes this does work, but no matter how cleverly disguised, it might convey a message similar to: "You didn't say 'yes' to our last RFP, so here's evidence that may help you change your mind on future hotel needs."

While this "traditional" practice of marketing is acceptable, it can be improved. Although educating customers is never a bad idea, information overload is making it harder to get your messages received, read and digested. Businesspeople today are over-mailed, stretched thin, and have little time to spare reading all the literature and electronic messages they are sent.

However, the second type of follow-up makes the first type much more effective. Dale Carnegie taught us *that to get what you want, first help others get what they want*. He said that if we live our lives helping others achieve their goals; everything we desire will come back ten-fold. We heartily agree.

"Treat others the way *they* want to be treated," is the mantra of this book. By blending the Carnegie philosophy with ours, salespeople learn to send goal-specific marketing messages that are readily received by prospective customers. If you took the time to Connect and Explore with those who did not award your hotel their business, you at least learned enough about their needs and expectations to have a better shot at earning their business in the future. That allows you to use high and low tech communication methods to send them articles, tips, and ideas to help them achieve their future goals and objectives. By sending customers helpful information about what is important to them professionally and personally, you will position yourself as a helpful, thoughtful professional, and not as a predatory salesperson. As Carnegie reminds us: *If you want to get everything you want, first help others get what they want!*

While performing our sales training, we are often asked if adapting to different styles and/or sending helpful information may be "manipulative." Our stock answer is, "It depends." If your intention is to help other people to make decisions that are in the best interest of their company and/or their career, then you are in no way practicing any form of manipulation. You are living The Platinum Rule. You are leveraging the power of persuasion in a positive fashion to create win/win outcomes in your business relationships. On the other hand, if your intention is simply to make a sale, mislead another person or do anything that is less than ethical, then we can confidently state you are using adaptability, technology, and persuasion in a manipulative fashion.

As Malcolm Gladwell pointed out in his best-selling book, *Blink*, almost every person has the innate ability to detect authenticity in another person in mere seconds. They do it on a subconscious level without even knowing they are doing so. If your intention is pure, customers and clients will subconsciously be compelled to want to do business with you.

Conversely, if your intention is to make money, push people into making buying decisions and/or manipulation, then no amount of training, psychology or technology will help you build a long-lasting career in sales.

CHAPTER 14

TAKE OWNERSHIP OF YOUR DESTINY

Imagine what would have happened if you had successfully applied the principles and practices of this book when first starting out in hotel sales? There are hundreds, if not thousands, of people like you that have already used these principles and experienced dramatic increases in sales volumes, and more satisfaction in their dealings with customers and co-workers. Many people report that they no longer feel like "just a salesperson;" they feel, behave, and are treated like a trusted advisor. They have an increased ability to help people find solutions to their problems and are more adept at identifying new sales opportunities.

For you to also share in experiencing these benefits, we encourage you to get started today. First, think about the goals you want to accomplish in the next week, the next month, or the next year! Then develop a plan to meet those goals using $uccessful Hotel $ales in 5 Easy $teps!

ACCEPT THE CHALLENGE

The first step requires your personal commitment to this challenge and belief in these platinum sales principles. Their success is proven and you can learn to put such principles to work for you. Of course, learning these new sills will take practice; you cannot realistically expect to put all of them into effect immediately. However, the minute you adjust your selling style to match the customer's buying style, you will start to see immediate results. We encourage you to accept this opportunity to strengthen your selling competencies!

MAKE A PLAN

Once you have accepted the challenge, you need a plan to incorporate these techniques into your life. Although we have provided you with an extremely simple, effective method of identifying and selling to the four behavior styles, it takes some practice. Start by trying to read the behavioral styles of those whom you know best: close business associates, friends, and family. Once you feel as though you have identified the styles of those you know, silently practice on the next prospective customer and adapt your sales approach accordingly. You will see a big difference in how customers respond to you in the future, making it easier to achieve, and even exceed, your sales goals.

COMMIT TO GROWTH

"Change is inevitable… growth is optional." We love that saying because it is true. Right now, you have the option to "finish the book" and get on with the rest of your life and career. After all, this is the last paragraph of this book. However, you also have the option to take this moment and make a life-changing decision. You may decide to keep learning about yourself: your strengths and weaknesses, your natural tendencies to react to both favorable and unfavorable conditions, how you make decisions, and how you project yourself to other people. You may decide to learn more about reading behavioral styles in your personal life. We have certainly found this to be true leading to improved understanding and relationship with our friends and loved ones. You will find this to be true over time, too.

Here's wishing you continued success!

Tony and Mick

APPENDIX

WORKSHEETS AND SUMMARY TABLES

The goal of these worksheets is to help you establish a clear understanding of the four behavioral styles. Once reading the behavioral styles of customers becomes second nature to you, it will be much easier to learn how to adapt your selling style to the behavioral style of the customer. By completing the four worksheets, you will maximize the potential of entering into a business relationship with each prospect you will encounter and reconnect with people you have been unable to sell to in the past. You will also find some great summary tables to help you adapt the way you sell to the way each of the four styles make purchasing decisions.

SELLING TO DIRECTORS

1. List five words that best describe the Director Behavioral Style:

2. What are three negative behavioral traits possessed by Directors that could make it difficult for you to successfully sell to them?

3. In what type of jobs, careers or positions might you often encounter Directors?

4. What are some things you need to know about Director customers if you are going to sell them on your products and/or services?

5. What are five key business characteristics of Directors?

6. What pace and priority should be used when communicating with a Director over the phone or in person?

7. What are five things you should do to help build rapport with a Director during your initial contact in the Connecting step of the selling cycle?

8. What are three things you should do to build rapport with a Director in the Exploring Stage of the selling cycle?

9. What are three things you should do to build rapport with a Director in the Collaboration Stage of the selling cycle?

10. What are three things you should do to build rapport with a Director in the Commitment Stage of the selling cycle?

11. What are five things you should do to build rapport with a Director in the Assurance Stage of the selling cycle?

SELLING TO SOCIALIZERS

1. List five words that best describe the Socializer Behavioral Style:

2. What are three negative behavioral traits possessed by Socializers that could make it difficult for you to successfully sell to them?

3. In what type of jobs, careers or positions might you often encounter Socializers?

4. What are some things you need to know about Socializer customers if you are going to sell them on your products and/or services?

5. What are five key business characteristics of Socializers?

6. What pace and priority should be used when communicating with a Socializer over the phone or in person?

7. What are five things you should do to help build rapport with a Socializer during your initial contact in the Connecting step of the selling cycle?

8. What are three things you should do to build rapport with a Socializer in the Exploring Stage of the selling cycle?

9. What are three things you should do to build rapport with a Socializer in the Collaboration Stage of the selling cycle?

10. What are three things you should do to build rapport with a Socializer in the Commitment Stage of the selling cycle?

11. What are five things you should do to build rapport with a Socializer in the Assurance Stage of the selling cycle?

SELLING TO THINKERS

1. List five words that best describe the Thinker Behavioral Style:

2. What are three negative behavioral traits possessed by Thinkers that could make it difficult for you to successfully sell to them?

3. In what type of jobs, careers or positions might you often encounter Thinkers?

4. What are some things you need to know about Thinker customers if you are going to sell them on your products and/or services?

5. What are five key business characteristics of Thinkers?

6. What pace and priority should be used when communicating with a Thinker over the phone or in person?

7. What are five things you should do to help build rapport with a Thinker during your initial contact in the Connecting step of the selling cycle?

8. What are three things you should do to build rapport with a Thinker in the Exploring Stage of the selling cycle?

9. What are three things you should do to build rapport with a Thinker in the Collaboration Stage of the selling cycle?

10. What are three things you should do to build rapport with a Thinker in the Commitment Stage of the selling cycle?

11. What are five things you should do to build rapport with a Thinker in the Assurance Stage of the selling cycle?

SELLING TO RELATERS

1. List five words that best describe the Relater Behavioral Style:

2. What are three negative behavioral traits possessed by Relaters that could make it difficult for you to successfully sell to them?

3. In what type of jobs, careers or positions might you often encounter Relaters?

4. What are some things you need to know about Relater customers if you are going to sell them on your products and/or services?

5. What are five key business characteristics of Relaters?

6. What pace and priority should be used when communicating with a Relater over the phone or in person?

7. What are five things you should do to help build rapport with a Relater during your initial contact in the Connecting step of the selling cycle?

8. What are three things you should do to build rapport with a Relater in the Exploring Stage of the selling cycle?

9. What are three things you should do to build rapport with a Relater in the Collaboration Stage of the selling cycle?

10. 1What are three things you should do to build rapport with a Relater in the Commitment Stage of the selling cycle?

11. What are five things you should do to build rapport with a Relater in the Assurance Stage of the selling cycle?

THE FOUR BASIC STYLES OVERVIEW

	Director Style	Socializer Style	Thinker Style	Relater Style
Pace	Fast/Decisive	Fast/Spontaneous	Slower/Systematic	Slower/Relaxed
Priority	Goals	People	Tasks	Relationships
Strengths	Administration, Leadership, Pioneering	Persuading, Motivating, Entertaining	Planning, Systematizing, Orchestration	Listening, Teamwork, Follow-Through
Growth Areas	Impatient, Insensitive, Poor Listener	Inattentive to Detail, Short Attention Span, Low Follow-through	Perfectionists, Critical, Unresponsive	Oversensitive, Slow to take action, Lacks global perspective
Fears	Being taken advantage of	Loss of social recognition	Personal criticism of their work	Sudden changes, Instability
Irritations	Inefficiency, Indecision	Routines, Complexity	Disorganization, Impropriety	Insensitivity, Impatience
Under Stress May Become	Dictatorial, Critical	Sarcastic, Superficial	Withdrawn, Headstrong	Submissive, Indecisive
Gains Security Through	Control, Leadership	Playfulness, Others' Approval	Preparation, Thoroughness	Friendship, Cooperation
Measures Personal Worth By	Impact, Results, Track Record	Acknowledgments, Applause, Compliments	Precision, Accuracy, Quality of Results	Compatibility, Contribution, Teamwork
Workplace	Efficient, Busy, Structured	Interacting, Busy, Personal	Formal, Functional, Structured	Friendly, Functional, Personal

STEP 1:
BUILDING RAPPORT DURING INITIAL CONTACT

Connecting with Relaters

- Relaters are Indirect and Open. However, keep the relationship businesslike until they warm up to you.
- They are concerned with maintaining stability; they want to know step-by-step procedures that are likely to meet their need for details and logical action plans.
- Organize your presentation: list specifics, show sequences, and provide data.
- Treat them with honesty, sincerity, and personal attentiveness.
- Listen patiently to their stories, ideas and answers.
- Express your appreciation for their steadiness, dependability, and cooperativeness.
- Present yourself to be non-threatening, pleasant, friendly, but still professional.
- Develop trust, credibility, and friendship at a relatively slow, informal pace.
- Communicate with them in a consistent manner on a regular basis… especially at the outset.

Connecting with Socializers

- Remember that they are Direct and Open.
- When you meet a Socializer, shake hands firmly, introduce yourself with confidence, and immediately show personal interest.
- Let them set the pace and direction of the conversation.
- Be an especially attentive listener with Socializers.
- Give them positive feedback to let them know that you understand and can relate to their visions, ideas and feelings.
- Tell humorous or unusual stories about yourself, to win their heart.
- Allow them to feel comfortable by listening to their stories, even to the point of talking about topics that may stray from the subject.
- Since Socializers typically enjoy talking about themselves, ask questions about them, but be prepared for lengthy answers. Plan to have as many meetings as necessary to build the relationship and gather information.

Connecting with Thinkers

- Thinkers don't care much about social interaction (beyond common courtesy and standard pleasantries), so get to the point.
- Avoid making small talk, except to initially establish your credibility.
- Speak slowly, calmly and economize on words.
- Thinkers are precision-oriented people who want to do their jobs in the best possible manner.
- Build your credibility by thinking with your head, not your emotions.
- Before meeting, provide them with a brief overview of the agenda and length of meeting, so they know what to expect.
- Show them logical proof from reliable sources that accurately document your quality, record of accomplishment, and value.
- Thinkers tend to be naturally suspicious of those who talk themselves up.

Connecting with Directors

- Directors want to know the bottom line.
- Just give them enough information to satisfy their need to know about overall performance.
- They do not want you to waste their time giving them a bolt-by-bolt description of your product, presenting a long list of testimonials from satisfied clients, or getting too chummy with them – always remember that they are Direct and Guarded.
- When you write, call, or meet a Director, do it in a formal, businesslike manner. Get right to the point. Focus quickly on the task.
- Refer to bottom line results, increased efficiency, saved time, return on investment, profits, and so on. In other words, tell him what's in it for him.
- If you plan to sell something or present a proposal to a Director, take care to be well organized, time-conscious, efficient, and businesslike.
- They do not want to make friends with you; they want to get something out of you if they think you have something of value to offer.

STEP 2:
MAINTAINING RAPPORT IN THE EXPLORING STAGE

Exploring with Relaters

- Relaters can be excellent interviewees.
- Talk warmly and informally and ask gentle, open questions that draw them out (especially around sensitive areas).
- Show tact and sincerity in exploring their needs.
- If they do not have a good feeling about you or your product, they are not likely to take the chance of hurting your feelings by telling you so.
- They want to avoid confrontations, even minor ones. So, Relaters may tell you what they think you want to hear, rather than what they really think.
- This same reticence may apply to telling you about their dissatisfaction with your competitors. Even though this is exactly what you want to hear, the Relater may be hesitant about saying anything negative about them.
- Allow for plenty of time for Relaters to open up to you and reveal their innermost desires and pains.
- The more time you spend Exploring with a Relater the higher the odds you will land them as a customer.

Exploring with Socializers

- Socializers get bored quickly when they're not talking about themselves.
- Strike a balance between listening to their life's stories and gathering the information you need to be an effective sales consultant.
- When asking business questions, keep them brief. If you can, work these exploratory questions in with social questions.
- The better your relationship with a Socializer is, the more willing he'll be to cooperate and talk about the task at hand.
- Socializers can be so open they may tell you their fondest hopes and aspirations. If you can demonstrate how your product or service can get them closer to their dreams, they may become so excited about your product—and you—that they're likely to sell you and your products and services to everyone else in their organization.

Exploring with Thinkers

- Thinkers don't care much about social interaction (beyond common courtesy and standard pleasantries), so get to the point.
- Thinkers often like to answer questions that reveal their expertise, so they can be very good interviewees.
- As long as you ask logical, fact-oriented, relevant questions, they will enjoy speaking with you.
- Phrase your questions to help them give you the right information.
- Ask open and closed questions that investigate their knowledge, systems, objectives and objections.
- Make your own answers short and crisp.
- If you do not know the answer to something, do not fake it. Tell them you'll get the answer for them by a certain time, and then do it.

Exploring with Directors

- To head off the Directors impatience before it surfaces, keep your conversations interesting by alternately asking questions and offering relevant information.
- Directors need to view a meeting as purposeful, so they want to understand where your questions are leading.
- When asking a Director question, make them as practical and logical as possible. Aim questions at the heart of the issue and ask them in a straightforward manner.
- Only request information which is unavailable elsewhere.
- When gathering information, ask questions showing you have done your homework about their desired results and current efforts.
- Be sure to make queries that allow him to talk about his business goals.
- Gear your exploration toward saving the Director time and energy.

STEP 3:
MAINTAINING RAPPORT IN THE COLLABORATING STAGE

Collaborating with Relaters

- Show how your product or service will stabilize, simplify, or support the Relaters procedures and relationships.
- Clearly define their roles and goals in your suggestions, and include specific expectations of them in your plan.
- Present new ideas in a non-threatening way.
- Provide them time to adjust to changes in operating procedures and relationships.
- When change becomes necessary, tell them why. Explain how long the changes will take and any interim alterations of the current conditions.
- Design your message to impart a sense of stability and security.
- Relaters like to be shown the appropriate steps to follow, so share those with them.
- Involve them by asking their opinions and encourage them to give you feedback.

Collaborating with Socializers

- Show how your product would increase the Socializers prestige, image, or recognition.
- Talk about the favorable impact or consequences your suggestions will have in making their working relationships more enjoyable.
- Give them incentives for completing tasks by stressing how their contribution will benefit others and evoke positive responses from them.
- Presentations need impact for people with short attention spans, so involve as many senses as possible.
- Show them how your solution will save them effort and make them look good.
- Back up your claims with testimonials from well-known people or high-profile corporations.
- Name some satisfied acquaintances that the Socializer knows and admires.
- Sprinkle in "visualizing future ownership" questions, such as: "If you were already running this software, how would you use it?" or "If this machine were delivered tomorrow, where would you put it?"

Collaborating with Thinkers

- Emphasize logic, accuracy, value, quality and reliability.
- They dislike talk that isn't backed up with both supporting evidence.
- Describe a process will produce the results they seek.
- Elicit specific feedback by asking, "So far, what are your reactions?" or "Do you have any questions that you'd like me to clear up?"
- Present your solution that shows them they'll be correct in making the purchase.
- Base your claims on facts, specifications and data that relate specifically to their needs.
- Thinkers are cost-conscious; increase their perceived value with facts and ROI data.
- Thinkers are the likely to see the drawbacks, so point out the obvious negatives before they do. Let them assess the relative costs-versus-benefits, which are typical trade-offs when making choices between competing (yet imperfect) products or services.

Collaborating with Directors

- Your presentation must be geared toward the Directors priorities.
- Gear your presentation toward how they can become more successful, save time, generate results, and make life easier and more efficient; you'll get their attention.
- Zero in on the bottom line with quick benefit statements.
- They want you to do the analysis and lay it out for them to approve or reject.
- Directors like rapid, concise analyses of their needs and your solutions.
- Directors like being in control, so give them choices backed with enough data and analysis to allow them to make an intelligent decision.
- Then, be quiet and let them make their decision. If you speak or interrupt while they are buying, you will dramatically decrease the odds of making this sale.

STEP 4:
MAINTAINING RAPPORT IN THE CONFIRMING STAGE

Confirming with Relaters

- Relaters are slower, deductive decision makers.
- Relaters listen to the opinions of others and take the time to solicit those opinions before making up their minds. So, make a specific action plan and provide personal guidance, direction or assurance as required for pursuing the safest, most practical course to follow. Arm them with literature, case studies and any documentation you have available, because they will be "selling" your proposal to others within their organization.
- When you do reach an agreement, carefully explore any potential areas of misunderstanding or dissatisfaction. Relaters like guarantees that new actions will involve a minimum risk to their desired stable state, so offer assurances of support.
- Try not to rush them, but do provide gentle, helpful nudges to help them decide (when needed). Otherwise, they may postpone their decisions.
- Involve them by personalizing the plan and showing how it will directly benefit them, their co-workers and the company as a whole.

Confirming with Socializers

- Show how your product would increase the Socializers prestige, image, or recognition.
- Be open and ask, "Where do we go from here?" or "What's our next step?"
- If they like something, they buy it on the spot (all other things being equal).
- You may have to slow them down because they also tend to overbuy and/or buy before weighing all the ramifications; behaviors that both of you may live to regret.
- Socializers dislike paperwork and details so they are likely to hesitate, and even procrastinate, when it comes to spending the time required on a contract.
- While a handshake is usually good enough, have a written agreement prepared due to their tendency to be unclear about procedures, responsibilities and expectations.
- Make sure that you agree on the specifics in writing or, later on, you can almost bet on some degree of misunderstanding and/or disappointment.

Confirming with Thinkers

- Emphasize logic, accuracy, value, quality and reliability.
- Provide logical options with appropriate documentation.
- Give them both time and sufficient data for them to analyze their options.
- They are uncomfortable with snap decisions and when they say they will think about it, they typically mean exactly that!
- However, if pressured by people or excessive demands, they may use "I'll think about it," as a stalling tactic in coping with such stress.
- Thinkers are educated, logical "shoppers." Know your competition so you can point out your advantages relative to what they offer. Thinkers are the most likely to do their own comparative shopping, so mention your company's strengths as you suggest questions they may want to ask your competitors.

Confirming with Directors

- With Directors, you come right out and ask if they are interested. A Director will often tell you "yes" or "no" (in no uncertain terms).
- You can easily lose the attention and/or interest of a Director by presenting your information too slowly or by spending too much time discussing minute details.
- When you draw up a commitment letter, be careful not to spend too much time on points the Director may not care about.
- Present them with options and probable outcomes. Directors like to balance quality with cost considerations, so offer options with supporting evidence and leave the final decision to them.
- We have found that it is effective to present a Director with two or three options. Provide a short summation of each option, along with your recommendation of each.
- While the Director is reviewing your proposal, don't interrupt them. The odds are high that they will find an option that appeals to them and closing the deal themselves.

STEP 5:
MAINTAINING RAPPORT IN THE ASSURING STAGE

Confirming with Relaters

- Follow-up consistently with a Relater.
- Give them your personal guarantee that you will remain in touch, keep things running smoothly, and be available on an "as needed" basis.
- Relaters like to think they have a special relationship with you; that you are more than just another business acquaintance; they prefer a continuing, predictable relationship.
- Give them your cell number, along with an invitation to call you any time with any concern. They will rarely use it, but will feel secure knowing it's available to them.
- They dislike one-time deals, so follow up to maintain your relationship.
- Impersonal, computerized follow-up is not very appealing to Relaters, so continue building your relationship with low-key, personalized attention and assistance.

Confirming with Socializers

- Socializers frequently buy before they're sold which may lead to buyers' remorse.
- Socializers can benefit from ongoing reminders that they have made the right decision.
- Reinforce their decision by giving plenty of assistance immediately after the sale.
- Be certain they actually use your product or they may get frustrated from incorrect usage and either put it away or return it for a refund.
- Since they mingle with so many people, you can even ask Socializers if they'd be willing to share their glowing testimonials about you and your product with others.
- If they are feeling smart for using your product or service, most Socializers will give you more referrals than the other three styles combined!

Confirming with Thinkers

- Set a specific timetable for when and how you will measure success with the Thinker. Continue proving your reliability, quality and value.
- Make yourself available for follow-up on customer satisfaction and ask for specific feedback on the product or service performance record.
- If you have tips for improved usage or user shortcuts, email them to your Thinker customers.
- You should also ask for their ideas and opinions for how to improve your products and/or services.
- When they offer you their suggestions, get back to them about how your company is incorporating their ideas into upgrades into future upgrades, revisions or new products.

Confirming with Directors

- Directors usually do not look for personal relationships at work due to their focus on accomplishing tasks.
- With "D's," do not rely on past sales to ensure future purchases. Follow up to find out if they have any complaints or problems with your product. If they do have complaints, address them immediately.
- Impress upon your customer your intent to stand behind your product or service.
- Stress that you will follow-up without taking much of their time.
- You may also want to offer a money-back guarantee.
- Whatever the promise, make sure you deliver everything you offer!

ABOUT THE AUTHORS

Dr. Tony Alessandra helps companies turn prospects into promoters. He is two speakers in one... a professor and a performer, or as one client put it – he delivers college-level lectures in a comedy store format. Dr. Tony offer audiences the opportunity to enjoy themselves while learning practical, immediately applicable skills that positively affect their relationships with prospects, customers, and co-workers. His focus is on how to create instant rapport with prospects, employees and vendors; how to convert prospects and customers into business apostles who will "preach the gospel" about your company and products; and how to out-market, out-sell and out-service the competition.

Tony Alessandra, PhD, CSP, CPAE

Dr. Alessandra has a street-wise, college-smart perspective on business, having been raised in the housing projects of NYC to eventually realizing success as a graduate professor of marketing, Internet entrepreneur, business author, and hall-of-fame keynote speaker. He earned a **BBA** from Notre Dame, an **MBA** from the Univ. of Connecticut and his **PhD** in marketing in 1976 from Georgia State University. He is also a prolific author with **30 books** translated into over 50 foreign language editions, including the newly revised, best-selling *The NEW Art of Managing People*; *Charisma*; *The Platinum Rule*; *Collaborative Selling*; and ***Communicating at Work***.

Dr. Alessandra was inducted into the **NSA Speakers Hall of Fame** in 1985. In 2009, he was inducted as one of the "**Legends of the Speaking Profession**;" in 2010-2015, he was selected as one of the **Top 5 Sales/ Marketing/ Customer Service Speakers** by Speaking.com; in 2010, he was elected into the inaugural class of the **Top Sales World Sales Hall of Fame**; in 2012, he was voted one of the **Top 50 Sales & Marketing Influencer**s; and in 2012, Dr. Tony was voted the **#1 World's Top Communication Guru**.

Dr. Tony Alessandra
DrTony@Assessments24x7.com • 1-619-610-9933
www.Alessandra.com • www.Assessments24x7.com
www.DrTonyVirtualTraining.com

Joseph "Mick" La Lopa, PhD

Professor La Lopa teaches sales, human resource management, and event & meeting planning courses in the School of Hospitality and Tourism Management at Purdue University. He earned his Ph.D. at Michigan State University (Go State!), his Master's at the Rochester Institute of Technology, his baccalaureate degree at the University of North Texas, and Associates at Richland Community College. He has taught thousands of students to have extremely successful careers in hotel sales.

Dr. La Lopa has a passion for teaching. He was the recipient of every major teaching award that can be bestowed to faculty members at the department, school, and university level in his first four years at Purdue. He was the 2003 recipient of the John Wiley & Sons Innovative Teacher of the Year awarded by the International Council of Hotel, Restaurant, and Institutional Educators. Dr. La Lopa shares his passion for teaching and learning with other educators by publishing papers, making presentations, and conducting workshops. Not only has Dr. La Lopa worked to improve the quality of teaching at Purdue University through various committees; he has been invited to deliver teaching and learning workshops for hospitality and culinary programs around the world, including Saudi Arabia. He is the originator of *Chef Educator Today* magazine, which at one point went to every secondary and post-secondary culinary program in the United States. He now does education consulting through the La Lopa Teaching and Learning Initiative he founded in 2012, which you can find on Facebook.

He has been happily married to his high school sweetheart since 1990. They have been blessed with 4 wonderful children.

You may contact Dr. La Lopa via email: lalopam@purdue.edu

www.ingramcontent.com/pod-product-compliance
Lightning Source LLC
Chambersburg PA
CBHW021559210326
41599CB00010B/512